Barefoot on the Prairie

Barefoot on the Prairie

Memories of life on a prairie homestead

Ferne Nelson

Western Producer Prairie Books
Saskatoon, Saskatchewan

Western Producer Prairie Books
Saskatoon, Saskatchewan

First paperback printing, 1991

Cover and interior illustrations by Joanne Oldring Sydiaha
Cover design by Warren Clarke/GDL

Printed and bound in Canada
10 9 8 7 6 5 4 3 2 1

The publisher gratefully acknowledges the support received from the Canada Council.

Western Producer Prairie Books is a unique publishing venture located in the middle of western Canada and owned by a group of prairie farmers who are members of Saskatchewan Wheat Pool. From the first book in 1954, a reprint of a serial originally carried in the weekly newspaper *The Western Producer*, to the book before you now, the tradition of providing enjoyable and informative reading for all Canadians is continued.

Illustrations are based on images taken from the author's family photograph album. Illustrations copyright © 1989 by Joanne Oldring Sydiaha, courtesy of Artworks, Saskatoon, Saskatchewan.

All illustrations in graphite on Arches.

Canadian Cataloguing in Publication Data

Nelson, Ferne, 1913–
Barefoot on the prairie: memories of life on a prairie homestead

ISBN: 0-88833-296-3 (cl.)
ISBN: 0-88833-355-2 (pb.)

1. Nelson, Ferne, 1913–. 2. Frontier and pioneer life–Alberta–Viking region. I. Title.
FC3667.2.N468 1989 971.23'3 C89-098100-0
F1076.N468 1989

Contents

Preface

In these little anecdotes, I have tried to give the reader a sense of what life was like when Alberta was very young. I wrote them because I enjoy recalling the events and conditions of those early days. If you are older, as I am, these stories may ring a bell in your memory, and I hope you will think: Yes, that's how it was.

I was born in 1913, and after so many years, my recollections may be faulty. In order to work in details of our daily lives, at times the truth is stretched a little; sometimes a lot. This seems to be necessary to give a fairly graphic picture.

All of our neighbours came from somewhere else, lured by the prospect of free land in a new country. Like my parents, John and Myrtle Alexander, they struggled and endured a very hard existence. As children were born, the ambitions of their parents shifted to them. I'm sure most of these hardy people succeeded. Alberta people are tough and durable, and every farmer is sure that next year will be better.

Bruce and Viking are still there. They haven't become metropolises, and I hope the people in those little towns like it that way. I now live in British Columbia, another beautiful province. But when I visit Alberta, I look up at that big, gorgeous blue sky and am glad that I was born there.

This book is dedicated to
the memory of my mother and father,
and especially Vera and Russell.

1

Child of a Log Cabin

I am a child of Alberta's prairies—strictly speaking, Alberta's grasslands. I was born in a log cabin on a poor homestead. My sister was born in a sod house, and when we were very young that house was still in use, though only as a chicken coop.

The prairie, crisscrossed with buffalo trails, stretched all around my parents' farm. Here and there bare bones of these magnificent animals bleached on the short, woolly prairie grass. The terrain was gently rolling, dotted with poplar bluffs, willow, and the occasional small, scrubby birch. There were frequent sloughs, some ringed with a white alkali deposit in dry weather. There were no roads, only trails, and very few fences. In travelling, one took the shortest route, hampered only by nature's boundaries.

When we were very young, no other children lived closer than four miles. Our lives were completely isolated, and all we knew we learned from our young parents. We saw other children sometimes on Sunday visits to neighbours, but in our daily lives, we played with each other and amused ourselves.

Life was hard. The seasons came and went. Winter, of course, was most cruel. Extremely cold weather was common, and with the northwest wind blowing, the temperature could drop to forty degrees below or lower. Then the two stoves were stoked continuously, and while we slept and the fires went out, the tin pail of drinking water in the kitchen would freeze over. On such mornings, the inside of the window panes sported a thick coat of fuzzy frost.

Spring was a joy. When the snow began to melt and the first bleached grass appeared on the little knolls, we took heart. The worst was over for that winter. Soon the first mauve crocuses would poke their shy faces through the ground, their fuzzy stems too short for even little fingers to pluck. Buffalo beans sprang up all over the sods that had banked the house for winter, their butter-yellow flowers contrasting sharply with the worn, grey logs on its south side. Tiny buttercups and violets were soon to follow, and from then on, there were many floral delights to be brought home to Mama. These treasures she would display in a broken teacup or well-washed tin can. A quart sealer of polliwogs from the slough would also decorate the window sill, though I cannot remember that we ever hatched any frogs. This was also the time of year when Mama would give us the dishpan and send us out to pick lamb's quarters, the first "greens" for the table.

As the warm days increased, as predictable as the first wild roses was the request, "Mama, can we go barefoot?" Barefoot we went. All summer and late into fall, shoes were forgotten. By threshing time our feet were tough and calloused. Not so in spring, when we left our boots behind and first ventured outdoors without them. Then our feet were lily-white, and we walked delicately, avoiding any rough places in the yard, watching carefully for broken glass, rusty nails, and all the debris that had sifted down as the snowbanks shrank.

Going barefoot on the farm had lots of hazards and many delights. One had to be careful in the barnyard—for obvious reasons—and there were slivers around the woodpile, as well as rocks where it was easy to stub one's toe. But the new grass was so soft and the mud around the slough squeezed up between the toes in such a satisfactory way that a child soon overlooked the disadvantages.

Our bare feet carried us into summer—a time of wild, sweet-smelling roses by the side of the road, ripe strawberries in the long grass, and saskatoons on the bushes by the coulee, a time for lying on Tidy's Hill and conjuring white clouds into ships and castles, adrift on a wide, blue sky-sea.

We always had some injuries to the toes and damaged nails in summer, but we loved going barefoot nonetheless. By autumn we could trudge along in the dust of the trail and it felt like silk underfoot.

Every summer night found us sitting on the back stoop, our feet in a basin of tepid water that became absolutely black as we washed off the dirt before going to bed. There was plenty of dirt to scrub off, for our day's play had taken us into many dirty places. Dirt is what farming is all about.

After harvesting, we generally went back to our shoes because we couldn't bear to walk on the stubble of the fields in our bare feet. Those sharp, hard spines were cruel to even well-weathered little feet. Soon school would start, and it would be shoes again until spring, when we could once more wriggle our toes in the soft, virgin grass.

I have no tales of high adventure. We had few thrilling experiences. Our lives were serene. Our pleasures were modest; our sorrows the same. We were as innocent as the violets in the pasture. Eventually we moved to town, and life became more sophisticated. The prints of our bare feet in the prairie grass lasted but a moment; the imprint of the prairies on our lives can never fade.

2

We Wanted Ice Cream

How had we got into this mess? Banished to the bedroom, our faces streaked with tears, we scraped away the frost on the little window and watched Mama struggling to hang the clothes on the line outside. The garments froze as her stiffened fingers fastened the wooden pegs. The long underwear and rigid petticoats whipped back against her body as she patiently pushed them back, stopping now and then to beat her cold hands against her sides.

Poor Mama. Life was hard on this prairie farm. She worked so hard, and today she looked so tired and worn. How could we have made fun of her just because she had become fat lately?

In fact, I hadn't even noticed it until my older sister had drawn that silly picture. Right now, I didn't like Ve. She had got me a stinging slap and a spanking. And Papa spanked hard. My little bottom still smarted. After all, I was only four years old, and Ve should have known better than to act smart and get us both into trouble!

Monday was always washday and so the big galvanized tub sat on two chairs in the middle of the kitchen. The sharp odour of yellow soap rose from the soiled laundry soaking in it. Steam swirled about from the wash boiler on the stove. Mama selected a couple of sticks from the woodbox, added them to the fire, and went back to the washboard. Her hair, which had broken loose from the combs that were meant to restrain it, hung limply about her face. She pushed it back with a soapy hand and scrubbed vigorously at a grey sock.

Outside, the March winds abused the tiny log house. The cold beyond and the steam inside combined to create a thick rime on the window panes. Ve and I amused ourselves by drawing pictures in the frost. Stars, cats, apples, and sunbursts sprang from our busy fingers.

"Look, Ve—I drew a horse." Ve drew a house and a tree. I put a bird in the tree and a flower under it. How nice it would be when spring came and we could play outside all the time, amongst real birds and trees and flowers!

We were bored. Mama had been irritable and impatient all day, and with the washing to do, had had no time to invent the usual little games. We were tired of our crayons and had quarrelled so much playing Snap that Mama had made us stop.

We continued our drawing, moving over to the other unblemished window pane. Ve drew a very fat lady with a big stomach and wispy hair. Underneath it she printed a word that I could read: MAMA. I laughed. It did look like Mama in her big apron with her hair all messy. We both dissolved in giggles. Mama looked up from the washboard and laughed too. She was happy to see that our boredom had disappeared.

Ve flushed with pleasure. She was amusing her little sister and showing off the sophistication she had acquired in a year at school.

"Mama is fat!"

"Mama is fat!" I echoed. I looked at my mother fearfully, sensing that I shouldn't have said such an outrageous thing. Mama hadn't heard us above the monotonous scrubbing.

"Mama looks like a fat old cow!"

"Mama looks like a fat old cow!"

We marched around the kitchen, turning the words into a sing-song chant. "Mama is fat! Mama is fat, fat, fat!"

Mama stopped scrubbing. A look of disbelief chilled her pretty face. Then she looked at the picture on the window.

Two girls were slapped hard. Two little girls and their mother burst into tears. Mama went back to the tub, her tears falling into the soapy water. We huddled in the corner, howling. We weren't slapped very often.

A gust of cold air warned us that worse was yet to come. That meant that Papa had come in from the barn. It didn't take him long to learn the cause of all the tears. He comforted Mama for just a minute before he administered two sound spankings and a warning that never again were we to ridicule our mother.

We were very subdued at supper and went to our chore of dishwashing without being told. We made a fairly good job of the dishes, without the usual wrangling. Ve washed and I dried. Mama sat in the rocking chair, knitting. She looked pale and tired and made no comment when we forgot two big pots in the warming oven.

Papa lit the lantern and trudged out to the clothesline. The wind still blew steadily, and he too fought the grotesque figures that our clothes had assumed as they hung like eerie ghosts in the dim yellow light. Soon the laundry was hanging all over the kitchen, and the old cookstove was roaring away drying all the chilly towels and sheets.

In the front room, we all clustered around the coal-oil lamp on the table. Papa read the *Free Press*, and we kids looked at the funnies. Tiring of that, we brought out our paper dolls, glamourous characters with beautiful clothes who lived an active social life of a kind that we had only heard about.

Papa read us an "Uncle Wriggly" story before we kissed our parents goodnight and went to bed. Shortly after that, they blew out the light and went to bed too.

Morning again. The weather was milder today. At breakfast, Papa said that a thaw was coming and that today we must go to Viking while the snow held for the sleigh. Mama cleared the table hurriedly and folded the dry laundry. She still seemed to be very tired and took a long time curling my blonde ringlets. Each one was carefully lifted and combed around her clever fingers. Then she braided Ve's dark hair in two thick plaits and tied them back with two blue ribbon bows. Doing her own hair, several times she laid down the brush and comb and sighed.

"Are you sick, Mama?"

"No, dear. Just tired. That big wash was just too much."

"Are you going to see the doctor?"

"Prairie Roses"

"Yes, dear. I will soon be better."

Papa tucked the buffalo robe tenderly around Mama's knees. Ve and I snuggled in the heavy blankets behind them, and we were under way.

Papa surprised us by driving into the Hansons' place and leaving us there to play with Karen and her younger sisters. We didn't want to stay, but felt better when Mrs. Hanson brought out cocoa and gingerbread.

It was dark when we heard the cutter in the lane. Papa was alone.

"Where is Mama?"

"She stayed at the hospital. The doctor said she must rest."

"Will Mama die?"

"Of course not. Mama said to be good girls. She will see you soon."

The days that followed were not pleasant. Days of lumpy porridge, burnt toast, and unaccustomed difficulties, of Papa trying to cope with unfamiliar tasks, and of all of us missing the one who made our tiny house a home.

Aunt Glad came on Saturday and baked bread and cookies, cleaned the house, and helped us with the weekend baths. The big tub came in again and now served as a bathtub. Auntie also washed our hair, but she wasn't as gentle as Mama and there were some tears and tangles.

Sunday, Papa went to town again. He returned alone. More tears and more questions. Mama was fine and would soon be well.

Another week of frustration and loneliness. We missed Mama so much. Did she go away because we made fun of her? If she would only come back, we would never, never do it again.

Wednesday. We struggled through another awful breakfast, cheered to learn that we were going to town to bring Mama home. Oh joy! Papa promised us a surprise in town. What could it be? New shoes, maybe. Our old ones were badly scuffed. Maybe oranges, or bananas cut from a long bunch in Schwartz's General Store, or even ice cream at Mrs. Brown's Ice Cream Shoppe, with the adorable little white tables and wrought-iron chairs.

It was a beautiful mild day. The sun shone on some red-winged blackbirds by Theaker's Slough. The snow had already melted in many places on the prairie. Old Cap and Prince had to be guided from one snow patch to another. In some places they had to pull the cutter over bare ground, and they strained at the traces. But Papa whistled and sang with us all the way to town.

The hospital wasn't really a hospital—it was just a big, comfortable old house where Mrs. Bishop provided a place for sick people to be near the doctor. We sat on the hard chairs in the little parlour and waited for Mama to get dressed.

The parlour door opened. In came Mama, looking rested and, although we didn't know the word then, radiant. Mama was well. She hugged and kissed us. Papa had to reach around us to kiss her.

Mama went back into the bedroom for the surprise. She brought it out carefully—a bundle wrapped in white. She folded the corners of the shawl back proudly to reveal a little, wrinkled, red face that opened up in a mighty yell!

In time we learned to love him. But on that day, we would have preferred new shoes, bananas, ice cream—anything to a new baby brother!

3

Kennedy's General Store

When we were little kids, Papa and Mama went to Bruce to do their shopping. Shopping was different then: people went to town to buy the essentials, not to browse through the stores. There was only one general store in Bruce, and it dealt only in basics. Its customers weren't browsers; they were farmers and townspeople who could afford only the bare necessities. Kennedy's General Store was there to supply their needs.

Everything you have heard about the old-fashioned store held true here. There really was a cracker barrel and a big round cheese on a board, a bunch of bananas hanging from the ceiling, and a tortoise-shell cat curled up somewhere. The cat preferred the pot-bellied stove in winter, but in summer she sought out shady places.

A big roll of heavy brown paper was installed at one end of the counter, and beside it was a cone of white twine, threaded through a clever little slot to keep it unwinding smoothly.

The shelves were stocked with sugar and flour, tea, beans, raisins, prunes, and salt and pepper. There was lard in bright red tin pails, Roger's Golden Syrup, Squirrel Peanut Butter, and various kinds of jam. There was coffee in an intriguing can labelled "Wedding Breakfast" that showed an enchanted bride and groom sipping the brew. On their table sat a can of the same coffee, picturing the same couple, and on and on. This label fascinated me.

There was a modest supply of drugs: Dodd's Kidney Pills, Zam Buk, castor oil, Epsom salts, Baby's Own Tablets, camphorated oil, aspirin, Sloan's Liniment, and Castoria.

One section of the shelves held Royal Crown soap, Sunlight soap, and Reckitt's blueing in little square cubes—everything for the weekly wash. And if a woman needed a new washboard for the endless scrubbing of dirty socks and overalls, Kennedy's had one. They knew what their customers needed.

Miss Olive Kennedy ruled over the dry-goods section. She had a few bolts of the kinds of material in demand: calico, broadcloth, denim, flannelette, chambray, cheesecloth, serge, and percale. If Mama wanted a few yards of cloth, Miss Olive measured it out in a fashion you would never see today. While her experienced fingers held the cut end of the material to the end of her nose, she stretched the cloth out to arm's length—that was a yard. Keeping her fingers at the yard mark, she transferred that place in the cloth to her nose and repeated the performance until Mama's five yards of broadcloth were measured. Then the material was cut on the counter, with the big scissors. No one ever questioned the yardage; we all knew that the distance from Miss Olive's nose to the end of her outstretched arm was a yard, wasn't it?

Mama did a lot of sewing, and watching Miss Olive measure the goods was one of our shopping pleasures.

While Mama went through her neatly pencilled list in Kennedy's, Papa picked up some other things. It might be a few sacks of hard coal for the greedy cookstove at home or some binder twine. He usually made a trip to the blacksmith's shop to have some bit of harness or farm tool repaired by Old Joe, whose hammer could be heard ringing on the anvil all over the little town.

After filling Mama's needs in the dry-goods department, Miss Olive would go to the back of the store to function in her other role, that of postmistress. She dispensed stamps, money orders, postal notes, and the mail with the same self-confidence she displayed in selecting thread and needles and knitting wool.

In the Post Office, there was the mail to get. Miss Kennedy deftly shuffled through a pack of letters while our mother watched hopefully. There might be something from her relatives in the States. Mama had lots of aunties, uncles, and cousins in various parts of the U.S. Although her father's continuous wanderings had brought his children to Canada, these relatives were still much interested in the welfare of their motherless nieces and nephews.

Sometimes there was a parcel from Eaton's, and usually the *Winnipeg Free Press* or the *Prairie Farmer.* We kids looked forward to the paper, with its funnies and Uncle Wriggly stories.

Russell Kennedy would have totalled up the bill by now, deducting the value of several dozen eggs and several pounds of butter that Mama had brought in. If we had any cash, he would be paid; if not, the bill would be filed on a spike behind the counter. There were lots of bills on the spike to be paid in the fall when the crop came in.

The groceries went in a cardboard box, and we knew that the kindly grocer had added a bag of candy for the kids somewhere in it.

If we had a nickel or a few pennies to spend, we would run up the sagging boardwalk to the "Chinaman's." He had a fascinating selection of candy in big glass jars on the counter: licorice sticks, horehound lozenges, raspberry drops, chocolate drops, molasses kisses, jawbreakers, maple buds, Cracker Jacks, and dozens of other kinds of candy. How could a kid decide? Hop Sing didn't hurry us in our selection. We took all the time we needed, and when our choice was finally made, the sweet old fellow usually tucked an extra goody into the little brown bag.

When all the shopping was finished, it was time for a quick snack at the Royal Cafe before the long drive home.

Old Cap and Prince, tied to the hitching post in front of Kennedy's had long since cleaned out their feed bags. Papa had taken them to the town pump where they had drunk greedily and noisily. The water supply in Bruce was slightly salty and didn't do much to slake a thirst. The horses would have to wait for a good drink at home.

Now that the team was untied, Rover sprang up from the back of the democrat where he had been sleeping and avoiding the town dogs.

Papa loaded the groceries and his family, and we set out for the seven-mile drive home. We kids were reluctant to leave the attractions of the town, but leave we must. Past the few houses, past the school and the empty Stampede grounds, past Idaho Pete's dirty old shack, past Gibbon's slough and Brown's Dairy. Soon the railroad station and the grain elevators faded from sight behind us.

4

Auntie Glad Makes Her Choice

It was a warm, bright spring day, and Mama and I were in the kitchen with the door wide open. I was "helping" Mama—a reluctant five-year-old dispiritedly pumping the dasher of the wooden churn. The action of the heavy handle made my little arms ache, and it seemed as though the cream would never turn to butter.

Mama was ironing. The ironing board was propped across the backs of two kitchen chairs, and my mother rotated the heavy irons, transferring the handle from number one to two to three as each became cold. The old McClary stove, newly polished with stove blacking, roared away, and perspiration streaked my mother's face as she smoothed petticoats and pinafores. She was working at top speed because the baby, bathed and powdered, was asleep and, therefore, undemanding. Perhaps these two jobs could be finished before he woke.

At this point I despaired of ever hearing the swishing, watery splash that would have indicated the cream was turning to butter. But Mama urged me on.

What I really wanted to do was go out in the yard and work on my mudpies. I had a nice line of them baking in the sun on the south side of the house, and I was anxious to get on with my grimy baking.

The two riders who came into view through the open door were a very welcome diversion. They were approaching from the north, and even at a distance, we were able to recognize Auntie Glad because the sun was on her shiny red hair. Her companion we didn't recognize, even when the pair drew closer.

I stopped churning and stood in the doorway, trying to guess who was coming with Auntie Glad.

Lately, Mama had been making plans for her young sister. In the evenings, while I covered my little blackboard with figures and drawings and letters, Mama and Papa talked. I heard these plans, and, while not fully understanding, I knew that Mama hoped that Auntie would get married to Mac McLeod.

Glad had visited us a few weeks ago, and Mac had come over with his shiny new vehicle and matched black horses and had taken Glad buggy-riding. They were gone a long time, came back very happy, and made plans for another outing on Sunday.

My aunt's creamy complexion was covered with rosy blushes when they returned from their second date. That was when Mama's hopes began to rise.

Ve was boarded out that year, as Papa and Mama were finally forced to do something about their tiny eight-year-old's schooling. So she wasn't around to explain things to me. But from the snatches of grown-up talk I heard when Auntie Glad went back to Lavoy, I pretty well got the picture.

After quitting school at an early age, our aunt had been working out as a hired girl, and Mama had been worrying about her. Mama suspected that her pretty younger sister was getting a bit "wild" and wished that she would settle down. In Mama's world, that meant to marry some decent man and assume the status and demeanour of a respectable married woman. Or at least, I heard my mother tell my father, Glad should go back to high school, finish her education, and maybe become a nurse or a teacher.

After Glad met Mac McLeod, Mama's hopes really took off. If this match was made, Glad would have a nice steady husband—one Mama highly approved of. Her flighty days would be over, and, presumably, they would all live happily ever after.

At night, by the light of the coal-oil lamp, Mama darned socks and sewed on buttons while she ran through Mac's qualifications again so that Papa would realize the chance Glad would have if she could lead this middle-aged swain to the altar. Mac was the school teacher in the neighbouring district—steady and with an assured income. Of course, he was much older than Mama's sister, but this was thought to be an advantage. He would "steady down" his youthful bride, and she would no longer be chasing off to dances and taking up with some of the carefree returned soldiers who were coming home from the war in increasing numbers.

After all, Mac was a good friend of my parents, and they knew he was of good character, reliable, and honest. He would make an ideal husband. Mama forgot I was there as she ran over the advantages of this match, and I listened carefully so that I could tell Ve all about it when she came home for the weekend.

The idea of having this kindly fellow as an uncle really appealed to me, and I knew Ve would like it too. Mac brought us treats and played games with us. In the winter, he took us sleigh-riding. Being tucked under the buffalo robe in the red cutter, with the bells ringing on his spirited horses, was our idea of "Dashing through the Snow" come true!

The two riders drew near the barbed-wire gate, let themselves through, and tied their saddle ponies to the fence post. Long auburn hair streamed out behind her as my aunt raced up the path and into my mother's arms. She was laughing and talking a mile a minute—and holding out her left hand to show Mama a shiny wedding band!

Her companion stayed behind, nervously fingering the horse's bridle. He was big, he was handsome, and he was dressed in khaki.

Mac McLeod never did marry. Was he really serious about my pretty red-haired aunt? Did his hopes collapse along with Mama's? Glad and our new uncle went up north to farm, and Mac went back to squiring the other single girls to the dances and picnics. He continued to visit us, looking and acting the same as ever, not at all like a broken-hearted lover. But Mama always believed that Aunt Glad was the girl of his dreams.

5

Broken Dreams

I didn't see a lot of Uncle Verne when I was growing up. He was the eldest of Mama's brothers and was married while I was still quite young. He went to live near his new in-laws at Lavoy and was busy with his farm and his family. While Forrest roamed the countryside on his pony, Lester stayed with us, and Auntie Glad sulked her way through school, Verne conscientiously went about raising a family and building his future.

The infrequent times when I did see my uncle, I was somewhat unfriendly to him. Certainly he was a nice man: mild, kind, and with all the attributes of a favourite relative. But, in my childish heart, I felt he had committed an almost unforgivable sin, a crime I couldn't put out of my mind: He had broken my doll!

It wasn't that I was that fond of dolls. I didn't play with them much and most of them I gave away, but I would never have parted with that little dolly.

This was a very special doll—a real treasure. My young mind wouldn't have been able to put it into words, but the tiny china figure was a pledge, a promise, a membership card, if you will, in the club I longed to join.

From the first time I held a crayon, chalk, or pencil in my tiny fingers, I wanted to go to school. Every scrap of paper that came my way, my little blackboard, or even the dust in the yard was covered with scribbles and scrawls, drawings, numbers, lines, and squares. I was a prolific "writer," and every visitor to the homestead was subjected to an exhibition of my skills as I showed off—blonde curls bobbing—an endless procession of ABCs.

When Ve started school at eight, I was five years old, still too young, and I was desolate. Mama and Papa explained that I had a year to wait. Although the days stretched ahead like a long road with no end at all, my preparations for the big day increased rather than slackened. I was so busy partly because Ve was boarding away from home and I had to amuse myself. Mama's patience was sorely tried. Busy with my new baby brother and dozens of household jobs, she was pestered all day long by my endless requests for more instruction, more help in reading the words on labels and jars. Like a sponge, I sopped up every bit of schooling that passed before my round brown eyes.

I got the doll at the Christmas concert. She was made of china, only about five inches tall, and was certainly a cheap little thing. She didn't even have clothes. Those were painted onto her body. She had big blue eyes and blonde hair and a white dress trimmed with rosebuds. I remember her well, but her life with me was very short—only about two weeks.

From her painted hair to her painted black Mary Janes, she was perfection. Not because of her beauty. No, indeed. She was a gift from the SCHOOL. In the way that the annual Christmas concert was organized, I suppose that every five-year-old girl at Rutherglen got one of those dolls from the tree that year. But no matter. To me, that little toy was recognition of my existence. The school knew about me! I would soon become part of it.

I cuddled and hugged my Flossie. Santa's gifts were loved and cherished, but the doll was everything. "I am coming, School. You gave me this dolly. You are going to welcome me to the place where I want to be. Soon I can explore the books, write on the big blackboard, finger the magical scribblers and plasticine, have a reader of my very own, and learn, learn, learn!"

On New Year's Day, Mama invited all her absent siblings to dinner. Our tiny house was crowded with the guests. Dressed in our best, we children circulated amongst our uncles and aunts, showing our Christmas gifts and enjoying the attentions of our relatives. And somehow in all the excitement of the day, I became careless and left Flossie on a chair.

Poor Uncle Verne. Flossie smashed into dozens of pieces when he sat down on her painted body. Papa said that no amount of glue could ever repair her damaged figure. Sobbing uncontrollably, I gathered all the little china bits and put them in a bottom drawer. My membership card was gone—my gift from the most respected institution in my life was smashed. The school had given me this beautiful dolly, and I had let her get broken.

Uncle Verne was probably the most admirable of my mother's brothers. He was always kind and loving to me. But for many years, the mention of his name always brought the same nagging memory to my mind. Uncle Verne—you broke my doll!

6

It's About Time

Oh joy, it was here at last! All through the warm and verdant summer, my heart sang with anticipation of September and my big day. Everyone I came in contact with was informed, endlessly, and Mama and Papa were tired of questions about school.

Mama had sewn new dresses for Ve and me. Mine was brown-and-white checked gingham with a white collar, and it hung in the wardrobe ready for the first day of school. I had two new pencils, two new scribblers—one with lines, one plain—and a box of wax crayons. I fingered them over and over. I could scarcely leave these treasures alone, but they had to be pristine and unused.

Two new lard pails, carefully washed and scalded, were ready too: one for Ve and one for me. They would be packed on the morning in September when we would set forth for Rutherglen School and a new term.

Finally it came. Papa hitched Duke and Fanny to the buggy and drove us as far as Theaker's corner, where he left us and hurried home to all his chores. We set out on the mile walk to the school. Straight down the dusty road. No loitering. No attraction could interrupt my progress. I just couldn't wait.

Beyond the barbed-wire fence, in Theaker's pasture, there was a horrible sight—a great pile of rotting cattle carcasses. The stench was overpowering, and we hurried on to get away from such a revolting scene. Ve told me these were John Theaker's cattle that had died in the hard winter. "Hard winter'' meant that the season had been long and cruel and that many farmers had run out of feed for their animals; the poor beasts died from malnutrition and exposure. John Theaker wasn't the only one who lost livestock. Many were the stories of the hard winter of 1918.

So here we were at the school, with some kids already milling around and playing a game of Auntie-I-Over over the schoolhouse. Mrs. Bender was already inside at her desk as we tiptoed into the cloakroom to put down our lard pails. Out in the yard we greeted the other children, most of whom we already knew.

Sitting by the south wall was poor little Bergit, who had been deposited there by a busy father. She was crying. The cause of her distress was soon apparent. She could speak not one word of English. She had spoken Norwegian from her first word, and here she was, ready for grade one, not understanding a thing that was said to her. Bigger girls sought to comfort her, and she dried her eyes, but still looked like some terrified small animal.

Mrs. Bender came to the door and rang her little bell. ''Children, line up in a nice straight line. Let us sing a song as we march in. Do any of you know 'Smile Awhile'?''

Some did, so we all formed a line and the teacher led us in a popular song of the First World War.

I watched Bud Lawes as he sang lustily.

''Smile the while I kiss you Sadadoo.''

Who is Sadadoo?

''When the clouds roll by I'll cumtuyoo.''

How does one cumtuyoo?

Well, I tried. I didn't know that song. Neither did Ve.

Inside the tiny one-room school, Mrs. Bender quickly assigned seats. There were four new grade ones, and we found ourselves in the smallest desks up front. I could open the lid of my desk and put in my scribblers. I looked over my desk with great satisfaction. Mine. It was old and bore the marks of many former students, but no matter. I explored the inkwell in the corner of the desk top. How soon could I write in ink?

Now that Mrs. Bender had all the students seated, we all stood for a morning prayer—"Our Father"—and "God Save the King." Mrs. Bender took Bergit on her lap while she welcomed us to a new term, and she promised that if we worked hard we would all do well.

I was pleased to find that Ve's desk was right across the aisle from mine. She gave me a smile. It meant that whatever happened at school, she would always be on my side.

Mrs. Bender had lots to do on the first day in her tiny school. She quickly made up an attendance roll and established the eight grades she had in her care.

I sat in my little desk, just savouring the moment. School at last! I sniffed the air—that unmistakable schoolroom odour, a mixture of chalk dust, ink, fresh paper, and children. My bare feet felt cool and comfortable on the freshly-oiled floor. The clean odour of the oil added to this olfactory treat.

We got our new readers. While Mrs. Bender was busy with other classes, I fingered mine most happily. I was pleased to see some familiar script on the first few pages. Then it changed to print like in Papa's newspaper. What was this? There was a list of my familiar ABCs, and underneath each was a letter something like it, only a little different. The rest of the reader was in print, not the sort of writing I had learned from Mama.

In the following weeks, we learned to cope with the reader and soon were reading: "Apples, apples, fine red apples. Will you have one? Will you have one?" in print.

Our teacher charged us all to help little Bergit with her language problem, and we spent most of our recesses and noon hours marching her around and teaching her the English word for everything in sight.

I revelled in the plasticine, the little cards with punched holes where one could sew a picture with a blunt needle and some yarn, the paper strips to weave into squares, the blunt scissors, the new chalk, everything!

I loved every minute of school. My scribblers were already sprinkled with gold stars, and I was trying very hard to become "Teacher's Pet." Mrs. Bender didn't have any pets, but I didn't know it then.

Mama and Papa would have been surprised and amused if they could have seen how industrious I was at school, because at home I was lazy about my chores. Here I became a thorough classroom pest, always begging Mrs. Bender for more work. I offered to clap the brushes, clean the blackboards, water the plants, tidy the bookshelves—anything. I'm sure the poor woman often wished I had started school somewhere else.

One day this over-eagerness to be helpful got me into my worst experience in grade one.

The schoolroom was empty that May day, except for my small six-year-old self. I stood, bare feet cool on the floor and stared at the clock on the wall. There was a faint sound of children's voices outside, but in the strangely quiet room, there was only the steady beat of the shiny pendulum and the rhythmic tick-tock, tick-tock. Mrs. Bender's desk was almost bare, except for a few books in a precise row against the ledge at the back and the bell that she had rung to start the school day.

The small desks we sat in from morning until afternoon marched in neat lines up the floor. The blackboards were clean—brushes stacked on the end of the ledge and chalk spaced evenly along the bottom. Mrs. Bender ran a tight ship, as one would say. The big roller map was shut in its box. Our artwork and pressed flowers decorated the walls. On the window ledges were house plants and a glass sealer containing a papery cocoon, soon to give forth a beautiful butterfly. A neat, one-room prairie school.

I stood gazing hopelessly at the big clock. I was very agitated. My small hands twisted the hem of my pinafore into a long knot, and my eyes did not waver from the shiny white face of the timepiece, where the thin black hands, like long slender darts, marked out the time of day. A big old wall clock. An octagonal frame circled its round, honest face. Big black Roman numerals marched neatly and, to me, meaninglessly around it. Below the candid countenance, the heavy pendulum swung back and forth, and the steady tick-tock was like a heartbeat.

The clock on the wall was there all the time, and in quiet

moments, we were aware of its soothing beat. But I had never been concerned with the actual time. My times were regulated by the grownups in my life. Mama and Papa announced bedtime, dinner time, time to start for school; Mrs. Bender rang the bell for class time, recess, lunch time.

That was good enough for me. Despite my thirst for knowledge, I had somehow never asked anyone to explain the mysteries of the clock's face. I knew my numbers. But the clock had X's and I's and a V thing like the first letter of my sister's name. It didn't really make sense. To me, it was just a clock, and we had one much like it at home, only smaller.

This May morning had started out very agreeably. Mrs. Bender had rung her little bell, just as usual, and we had lined up in front of the school, ready to march in to our desks. But this day our teacher said we would work in our garden before starting classes. This was a treat we all enjoyed. There was an orderly rush to get out the hoes and rakes before we all trooped across the schoolyard to our School Fair project.

The fair was the high point of the school year for us, and Mrs. Bender encouraged wholehearted participation. All year we drew maps, prepared artwork, pressed flowers and weeds, and collected butterflies while poring over the booklet that set out the various competitions. At home the older pupils hemmed dishtowels and made dusting mitts and aprons. Later on, as the big day drew near, there would be nerve-wracking sessions of baking and canning. I was still too young to try "plain cake—un-iced," but was anxious to do my bit in the school garden. Here we hoped to grow vegetables that would win lots of blue ribbons for Rutherglen School.

Under our teacher's direction, we hoed and raked. Already the biggest boys were starting to mark out neat rows with pieces of binder twine between two sticks. The precious free seeds were brought out, and tiny fingers learned to drop them ever so carefully into the furrows.

It was then, in the warm sunshine, with everything so right in the world, that a six-year-old—me—got herself into big trouble.

Mrs. Bender straightened herself from her bent position where she was showing Evelyn and Bergit how to tamp the tiny carrot seeds into the ground. She called me to her side. "Can you tell time?"

Quick as a flash I answered "Yes." I couldn't, of course, but if I was going to continue in my role as grade one "wunderkid," a negative answer was out of the question.

"Please, clock, tell me. What time are you?"

The clock ticked steadily on. Not a clue. There is a big hand here and a shorter hand there. What do they say? The pendulum beat out its measured orbit. The clock's face was pure, innocent, inscrutable.

Finally I realized I would have to fake it. Maybe, just maybe, I would be right. Those two marks, up near the top—I knew what they said. Hippity-hop back to the garden and the busy gardeners. Back to Mrs. Bender's side.

"Eleven o'clock! Good gracious, how the time has flown! We must pick up our tools. Quickly now. Come, children—we have to start our regular classes. I had not intended to spend so much time in the garden."

Back in our desks. Quiet. Waiting for Mrs. Bender to come in from the cloakroom, where she was still washing her hands.

My hands—wet, but not from washing—were in my lap. I was a nervous wreck. Mrs. Bender is going to look at the clock. Please, dear, dear clock. Be eleven. Please. Don't let me get caught in my lie. Please be eleven!

"All right, children, take out your work. Only an hour to lunch time and plenty to do. We will start with grade one reading."

The four grade one pupils obediently took out their brown readers. Our teacher juggled eight grades in her little rural school, and everyone knew his assignment.

"Page twenty-seven, class. Ferne, stand and read, starting at the top of the page."

Saved. I sprang to my feet.

Then Mrs. Bender looked at the clock.

She took off her glasses and looked again. My legs turned to jelly. I leaned on the desk to keep from falling.

Mrs. Bender was an excellent teacher. She was dedicated to her job, determined that this little flock of farm children would get the best education she could give them. The school had only the bare minimum of equipment. It was bare and draughty—nothing more than a stark building on the Alberta prairie with a few desks, blackboards, and a tiny library in the chimney corner.

Yet the pupils of Rutherglen learned quickly, moving confidently from grade one until they passed their grade eight exams with good marks. And it wasn't just books that added to our knowledge. We were encouraged to take an active interest in trees, flowers, weeds, insects, birds, and the animals around us. Mrs. Bender was strict, but fair. There was a strap in the drawer. It was seldom used, but I knew it was there. I had never been in trouble at school. Did my adored teacher strap little girls for lying? Never in my life had I been in such panic.

My big sister was in the room. She would tell. What would Mama and Papa say tonight?

All this was in my mind as, shaking in fear, I neared the teacher's desk. How could I explain that it was from a desire to please, to be useful, that I had lied?

Mrs. Bender put her hand under my chin, raising my downcast face until my eyes were forced to meet her stern gaze. If only the floor would open up and I could disappear beneath it.

"Ferne—it is now ten minutes past ten. I ask you again, can you tell time?"

Behind me the other children were tittering with amusement. The tears came now. Sobbing wildly, tears raining on my pinafore, I finally got it out.

"No, Mrs. Bender."

My teacher produced a clean white handkerchief and mopped my wet face and streaming eyes.

"Well, child, this is a good time to learn. Does anyone else in the room not know how to tell time?"

In the lower grades, a few timid hands went up.

All classes were suspended while we learned the mysteries of the big school clock. Mrs. Bender never let the curriculum interfere with practical concerns.

7

An Independent Business Woman

Any visitor was welcomed to our isolated farm, and Mrs. Krause was no exception. She came a couple of times a year, and in style, too, in a shiny black democrat buggy pulled by two lovely bays. I remember her as a sort of Queen Victoria, sitting regally on the front seat, holding the reins, and expertly controlling her spanking team. We kids rushed to open the gate for her. If Papa was around, he gallantly unhitched the horses, put them in the barn, and fed them. Meanwhile, the Rawleigh Company's representative took down her big black case and established herself in the house. She always timed her visit so she would be staying overnight with us.

We kids kept our eyes on the case. It didn't hold much interest for us, filled as it was with spices and medicines, but we looked forward to the time when she would open it and present her wares. That was when she gave us the chewing gum. Actually, we didn't like the gum nearly as much as the kind that came from the store in town. Rawleigh's gum was very bland compared to Wrigley's Spearmint or Doublemint or Tutti Frutti, but we surely didn't turn it down.

Mrs. Krause was a sweet little woman. Did I say little? Well—she had tiny hands and feet. She was short, too, but very stout. She really was a lot like the famous old queen. Dumpy, I guess. Well-corseted, but no rigid stays could control the rolls of fat around her middle. Her hair was strawberry blonde, piled high, and always very neat. It was held in place with beautiful tortoise-shell combs. Ve and I thought them very elegant and decided that when we grew up, we would have some exactly like them.

Our visitor sat in for supper. She enjoyed Mama's cooking and had second and even third helpings.

After supper the sample case was opened, and Mama got ready to make her selections. Black pepper, for sure. Rawleigh's pure vanilla extract—a big bottle. Lemon, too, but a smaller bottle. Cinnamon—Mama used a lot of that. Some other spices, especially some for pickles and rhubarb relish.

Then on to the medicines. Medicated ointment. If we got colds next winter, our chests would be rubbed with lots of that. Red liniment. We would get that in hot water (with cream and sugar) for stomachaches. And a big tin of carbolic salve for sores that wouldn't heal. This was sort of an all-purpose medication—Papa often used it on the barn animals. We must have that.

While our saleslady set out the selected items, Mama was mentally calculating the cost. She mustn't pick out more than she could pay for because cash was something we never had much of. A few more things, and the shopping was done. We didn't have to wait for delivery; Mrs. Krause went to her buggy and brought in the goods right then.

The sample case closed, we went on to our usual evening activities while the grownups caught up on the news. Mrs. Krause had been all over the neighbourhood recently and had all the gossip from those farms. We found most of it rather dull and went on with our homework or games or whatever.

Ve and I dreaded bedtime when the Rawleigh lady came. Oddly, Mama didn't ask us to sleep on the floor; our visitor slept in our narrow bed with us. This was very uncomfortable, and only our ability to sleep anywhere got us through the night. The portly little lady plunked herself squarely in the centre of the bed. The covers, draped over her ample shape, formed sort of a tent, and we little girls crawled in, one on each side of her, on the outskirts of the tent. We didn't like this situation as we hardly got enough quilt to keep us warm. The floor would have been better!

Morning, and the team was hitched to the buggy. Mrs. Krause and her precious case moved away across the prairie.

Tonight she would bed down with some other family. In six months or so, always depending on the weather, she would be back. She had a husband and a houseful of kids at home. In our world, all the other women stayed home, but she spent her days bumping over rutted roads, making a living. An early independent business woman.

8

Our Favourite Uncle Finds a Bride

I have to tell you about Uncle Forrest. While Lester struggled with all the problems of adolescence, Forrest really enjoyed life as a free spirit. He was full of the dickens, as they say, and was a born prankster and daredevil.

Forrest was small, blonde, and wiry, as were all Mama's brothers. He was footloose and unattached, a gay, carefree young blade with a superb saddle horse and practically nothing else in the world. He came and went at our home, sometimes helping Papa around the farm or sometimes hiring out to some other farmer. That he was undependable goes without saying. A few days of drudgery in the fields or barnyards and he was off on his pony looking for adventure.

Mama came home one day from one of her berry-picking expeditions, unaware that Forrest was anywhere around. She believed him to be miles away, but as she hurried to build a fire and get supper before Papa got in from the field, she remembered seeing a horseman disappearing over the ridge as she neared home. Her suspicions grew as the faithful old McClary erupted in clouds of smoke. The fire would not start, and the house filled with a dense smog as Mama lighted match after match and adjusted the dampers. Papa returned to a frustrated wife and a bare dinner table. He had to go up on the roof and remove a great wad of rags from the stovepipe before the meal could get underway.

We knew by this prank that our uncle was back from his travels. We youngsters adored him. He was just a big kid himself. When he was around, he played games with us, pulled the sled in the wintertime, and entered into endless games of hide-and-seek. He could make a wonderful whistle out of a slippery willow branch and fold a magical bird out of a piece of paper. He would push the swing for hours and then take a high-flying ride himself. Taking turns sitting behind him on his pony, arms tight around his waist, we had many a hair-raising ride over the prairie.

Poor Alfie provided Forrest with a victim for his practical jokes all one summer. Alfie was what was known as a "Green Englishman." He was newly arrived from England the summer that he hired on as a helper for Papa. He was, I suppose, from some city in the Old Country, knew absolutely nothing about farming, and was most anxious to learn. Forrest soon understood that the naive young fellow would believe anything he was told, especially if the information was passed on with a straight face and a seeming desire to be helpful. So our new hired man found himself in some pretty funny situations, like driving a lumber wagon all day with the wheels reversed or trying to milk a steer. He also believed that we got nice streaky bacon by feeding the pigs well one week and starving them the next.

After Forrest took Alf snipe-hunting, Papa put a stop to a lot of this mischief.

It was great fun, Forrest assured Alfie, to go out at night and get a bag full of snipes. They would work together. Alf was to station himself in an old slough bottom, with a big gunny sack propped open to form a trap. Behind the blind, all the Englishman had to do was sit with a lighted lantern while Forrest went off through the long grass to arouse the sleeping snipes. Attracted by the light shining through the sack, they would, presumably, walk right into the trap.

Alf did his part of the hunting, sitting all night with his lantern. Forrest, having instructed his pupil to sit motionless and wait for the tasty birds to fill the sack, went home to bed. At dawn poor Alf came home with an empty sack, tired and stiff from his long vigil. The thought of having to work all day in the harvest field after a sleepless night added to his misery.

Forrest really outdid himself in the case of Len Lawes. This time it wasn't planned and resulted mainly from Forrest's way of doing things. He really didn't mean to play a trick at all, but he surely spoiled a nice party.

Some of our neighbours were at our place celebrating the return of Len from overseas. Len, you see, was back from the First World War, in which he had been an unwilling participant. His experience in the holocaust had left him shell-shocked, as it was called in those days. But this was all forgotten as a few friends gathered to dance and sing and rejoice in his return.

That had to be the night that Forrest returned from somewhere. He arrived on foot, and being Forrest, it never occurred to him to come to the door and walk in. Instead, as he neared our place he saw the lights in the windows, and knowing that someone was still up, he thought of a spectacular way to announce his return.

He seldom went anywhere without his rifle, and he had it with him then. What better way to let his sister and brother-in-law know that he was home? As he entered the yard, he lifted his gun high, pointed it to the heavens, and fired off a nice loud blast.

Bedlam. Len Lawes, thinking that the Germans had somehow invaded Alberta, went into absolute hysterics. Everyone inside was immediately occupied with the resulting confusion. Women and small children cried as Len screamed and raved, while several men struggled to hold down the poor tormented soldier. Getting no immediate attention, our uncle continued to fire volley after volley in a vain effort to get someone out to welcome him. Over the din, Mama and Papa finally made themselves heard as they repeatedly shouted that it was Forrest.

The unfortunate soldier was finally subdued and lay sobbing on the couch. Papa finally found time to go out into the darkness and bring the culprit in.

Forrest was full of apologies, but the party was ruined.

I cannot say that this was the end of my uncle's pranks. I wouldn't even want to say it. Most of them were harmless fun, and there are few enough people in the world with his love of a joke and his ability to brighten the dull days on a lonely homestead.

But when he brought his bride to our house, the tables were turned on Forrest. The first we knew of it was when a lot of people appeared at our door one night. They were laughing and singing and banging on pots and tin cans.

Papa came out of the bedroom, hurriedly pulling on his pants. Mama was up too, lighting the kerosene lamp. The baby, disturbed by all the noise, was crying lustily. Ve and I were out of the blankets at once, running to the window.

The full moon shone on a most unusual sight. Saddle horses were tied to the fence, and there were buggies and an old lumber wagon too. One man was alighting from his horse, carrying a case of some kind. Old Rover was barking his head off, and the din was terrific. The people at the door were in a gay mood and demanded that Uncle Forrest come out.

Most nights in our lonely little house were absolutely silent, except for the soft neigh of a horse in the barn or, perhaps, the far-off lonely howl of a coyote. When the lamps were blown out, we knew that nothing would stir until morning.

That night, as usual, we had all gone to bed early. Bed, for Ve and me, had been on the floor in the front room because Uncle Forrest and our new auntie had our bed and our bedroom. We had no spare beds, so we kids had blankets and pillows on the floor. We didn't mind—we could sleep anywhere.

Uncle Forrest had brought his bride to our place about a week earlier. Mama and Papa said that Forrest and Hilda had eloped.

The elopement was the culmination of Uncle Forrest's seemingly futile courtship, which had been going on for a year or so. One day, while galloping over the prairie, he had noticed that the ploughman in Bruckhardt's field was a girl! The coarse overalls and heavy boots failed to conceal the fact that she was young and lovely. Thick, glossy brown braids were stuffed under her old felt hat. Although her face was streaked with dust, two beautiful blue eyes shone forth, only to be lowered bashfully when Forrest got off Paint and strode over the newly ploughed furrows to become acquainted.

In subsequent meetings in the field, Forrest learned more about this lovely creature. Her father, Mr. Bruckhardt, was blessed with three girls but no sons. He had counted heavily on boys to help him farm, and when no sons appeared, Hilda became the male child he had hoped for and spent her days ploughing, sowing, and reaping. She did all the heavy work that a man would have been expected to do around the farm.

Herr Bruckhardt, a German of the old school, demanded absolute obedience and forbade fraternizing with the neighbours. Besides, he was taking no chances on losing his number one farm-hand. So when from afar he spotted the resting plough or the grazing saddle horses, he took immediate, predictable action. He vowed that if he caught Forrest hanging around Hilda, he would shoot him on sight!

Such an announcement terrified his eldest daughter, but it was merely a challenge to my adventurous uncle. If Hilda had been attractive to him before, now she was doubly desirable and a prize that must be won!

As they say, love will find a way, and somehow the clandestine meetings continued. Hilda and her sisters were not allowed to go to the local picnics and box socials, so the trysts had to be arranged on the pretext of seeking a stray cow or mending a broken fence. Papa had remarked more than once that if any of our stock strayed, they always seemed to head in the direction of Bruckhardt's place.

So a week ago this love affair had culminated in the elopement. How this had been accomplished, we kids didn't know, but Forrest and Hilda were at our place to stay awhile. With youthful optimism, neither groom nor bride had looked beyond the marriage, and the blissful newlyweds lingered with us while they planned their next move.

Nothing had been heard from Mr. Bruckhardt and his meek little wife. Ve and I searched the faces revealed in the moonlight. How about that threat to shoot Uncle Forrest? Was Hilda's fierce old father out there?

Mama shoved us away from the window. We had to pick up our makeshift beds and take all the quilts into the bedroom, where Rus still cried and Mama tried to do up her hair. We were begging to put on our best dresses and asking dozens of questions.

There were no signs of life from the bedroom where the bride and groom were bedded down.

Now that Mama was dressed, Papa threw open the door and invited our surprise guests to enter. They burst in, full of high spirits and demanding the newlyweds. Some of the men pounded on the bedroom door.

"Come out, Forrest. We want to see the bride!"

A sleepy uncle finally emerged, to be subjected to much back-slapping and hand-shaking, congratulations, and good-natured joshing. The women, one by one, slipped into the bedroom and coaxed Hilda to come out.

After a long wait, she finally allowed herself to be pushed into the room, where, red-faced, she clung to her husband while she was kissed and congratulated.

Satisfied that Hilda's father was not in the group, we thrilled to this unexpected party. In the lamplight, our visitors were revealed as neighbouring farmers and their wives, the men shaved and scrubbed and the women all prettied up in their nicest dresses. There was lots of laughing and joking as they prepared to relieve the tedium of hard work and poverty with a night out.

Ford Merner opened his case and took out his fiddle. Somebody had an accordion, and Mama sat down at the piano. The floor was hastily cleared for dancing, and soon the tiny room was crowded with couples trying to find space to do a two-step or waltz. They even managed some square dances, with Charlie Haeberle calling the squares. Ve and I sat in the corner and watched the intricate patterns as they do-si-doed and swung their partners. We joined in the clapping at the end of each set and wished that someone would ask us to dance. Some of the men actually did ask us and held us at arm's length as we hopped around with complete disregard for beat or rhythm.

After a while some of the women got the coffee pot going. Parcels on the kitchen table were revealed as cakes, pies, doughnuts, and sandwiches that the guests had brought. The musicians announced that they needed a rest, and every chair and apple box and milk can we owned was called into service as the dancers sat down for refreshments. Ve and I were thrilled to pass the plates, helping ourselves generously after every round.

Then it was back to the dancing, and I never knew how long it lasted because, eventually, I stumbled into the bedroom and fell asleep on a pile of coats on Mama's bed.

Forrest and Hilda got a job soon after working on Ernie Manly's farm. We talked about the shivaree for days, even trying to incorporate it into our play house routine, but had to give up the idea. We lacked enough players to bring it off successfully.

Long after, when I was in high school, I ran across a strange word in my dictionary. "Charivari: a mock serenade of discordant music. Sounding it out carefully to learn the pronunciation, I found an old friend—my aunt and uncle's shivaree.

9

The Day Our Mothers Went to Town

The holiday wasn't completely ruined after all. The kids were still pale and thin, but feeling much better and well on the road to recovery. There were a couple of weeks before we had to go home. Only one small incident clouded the sunny outlook.

Still, Mama and Auntie bustled about, fixing an abundant meal for the two families and cheerfully ignoring the fuss they had caused. They tried to ignore the hostile stares of their husbands and the sobbing of my little brother. My sister and I and our three cousins had almost nothing to say; our affection for our mothers was mixed with the desire to please our fathers and side with them. Rus's reaction was strangest of all. The tears rolled down his cheeks as he insisted that that wasn't his Mama.

First Papa, then Uncle Herman would berate the guilty pair. How could they do such a thing? Didn't they know their husbands would not approve? What was the world coming to when wives acted so callously without their husbands' consent? Papa said that Mama would be the laughing-stock of the country when we got back to Alberta and the farm. Mama said she didn't give a darn.

Aunt Helen and our mother went on with supper preparations, smiling cheerfully and ignoring the tirade. Obviously they had anticipated this hostility and planned their reaction to it. From time to time, they tossed their pretty heads and threw out a few cheerful remarks about it being a free country and that they were old enough to know what they were doing. They served up the steak and mashed potatoes, called the kids to the table, and tried to establish our usual happy mealtime, but the men retreated to stony silence. In an effort to get away from the strained atmosphere, we six cousins ate quickly.

Looking back, the escapade the two women indulged in that day was a natural and inevitable result of several very trying weeks. They needed a break from housework, sick children, and isolation, and their action was as predictable as the snap of a tightly-coiled spring when the pressure is released.

We were visiting our relatives in the States for a couple of winter months. Since we were so chronically poor, the visit could happen only if Papa worked while we were in Idaho. His brothers had found him employment in the mill where they worked. However, there still should have been lots of time for visiting and fun. We had looked forward to the trip for a long time.

The train ride was long and tiring. No sleeper for us: we couldn't afford that luxury. We kids napped on our parents' laps or on an empty plush seat, but Mama and Papa got almost no rest. I got sick.

Mama was accustomed to my frequent stomach upsets, but on the train, I was also feverish, with a sore throat and watery eyes. Poor Mama did what she could to relieve my misery, but we were all happy to arrive at Aunt Helen and Uncle Herman's comfortable home. There, I was promptly put to bed.

Next day, the cause of my distress became apparent. I broke out in hundreds of spots from head to foot. Red measles! The quarantine card went up on the front door, and it was just a matter of time until the five other children succumbed to the disease. The miserable weeks dragged on as, one by one, we complained of the now familiar symptoms and developed the horrid spots. Our mothers, bone-tired, moved from one sick child to the next, carrying drinks, chamber pots, and hot water bottles and tending to the unending demands of

"Potatoes"

feverish, peevish, and often desperately sick children. They had little rest and no relaxation.

The men of the household were allowed to continue working at the mill, so Mama and my aunt spent the days in the company of their cranky children, acting as combination nurses, housemaids, and cooks. The pleasant visiting they had planned didn't materialize. They were thoroughly fed up with nursing and housework. Two tired men, returning from the mill after dark, did little to make the endless days any brighter.

The day the quarantine was lifted was liberation day. We children were all on the way to complete health. Even the weather was better. The sun shone forth with a promise of spring. The whole world looked brighter.

That was the day the two women made up for all their trials of the last six weeks. These two young women, loving mothers and respected wives, usually compliant with their husbands' wishes, proper in dress and deportment, did a very daring thing.

Their crime?

On this lovely warm and sunny day, my mother and Aunt Helen left their six children at home. While their unsuspecting husbands slaved away on the lumber piles, they boldly walked into town. There they entered a certain establishment and came away with their lovely thick hair bobbed and shingled!

10

Papa Finds a Way

The kitchen door opened, letting in an unwelcome blast of cold air. Papa stomped the dry snow from his buckled overshoes and stepped into the tiny room. Mama, flushed from the heat of the stove, was taking another batch of cookies from the oven. Sister and I barely looked up from our business of making red and green paper chains, but Rus ran to Papa with the same question he had been asking for several days.

"Will the Indian come?" Papa picked up his scrawny four-year-old and looked serious and concerned.

"I don't know, Rus. He could still come." But he knew, and we knew, that it was too late—the Indian wasn't coming.

Christmas Eve on an isolated farm in Alberta's grasslands. It was afternoon now. It would soon be dark, and the Indian hadn't come. The wind blew steadily from the northwest, not yet a blizzard, but it held a threat of stronger action, and the powdery snow was piling up ever so slowly around the exposed north doorway.

When Illinois-born Papa built our little house, he had, in his ignorance of Alberta weather, planned the kitchen door to face north. Every time it opened, old North Wind pushed in with all his might and Mama was always sweeping up his powdery deposits of snow inside the stoop. Even though it had been snowing and blowing off and on now since October and a huge drift protected the vulnerable doorway, each time someone passed through it, an icy draught chilled the tiny kitchen.

Just a little family, three kids and their young parents, protected from the weather by this little log house, the logs chinked with moss and mud to keep out the cold and the wind. Two hungry stoves that must be fed wood and coal round the clock, or everything inside would freeze. Forty below outside, tomorrow would be Christmas Day, and the Indian hadn't come!

My father had stood in line all night in Edmonton to file claim on this worthless homestead on the Alberta prairie. Its alkali soil begrudged every bit of nourishment it gave to the crops. They were planted so hopefully every spring and watched so optimistically through rain and sun, but were usually ruined by an early frost or a steady rain of hail that dashed my father's hopes for another year. Looking at the flattened fields, deep in ice pellets, he knew in his heart that he would never make it on this poor farm.

The uncultivated land was covered with scrubby poplars. They never recovered sufficiently from the cold winter to grow much in the summer, so they remained small and wizened. Willows ringed the little sloughs, and the silver willow, preferring a higher location, followed the gentle curves of the prairie. A few stunted birch tried vainly to add some grace to the landscape. Now all were bare, and the snow had shifted into drifts that nearly buried the smaller trees. Not quite the enchanting scene on a Christmas card. No gracious evergreens or bright holly. Lots of snow, though, and lots of love and expectation in the little house. But casting its shadow over the bubbling excitement of three children was the certain knowledge that the Indian wasn't coming.

On Christmas Eve, three children should have been asking if Santa was coming. But we knew he would come. Ve and I were wise to the Santa myth and had watched with satisfaction as the big bulky parcels arrived from Eaton's. Hadn't we studied the Fall and Winter Catalogue from the time it had arrived and greedily selected dolls, books, jewellery, and perfume, with the certain knowledge that we would receive very little on Christmas morning? Rus took an active interest in the toy section, not quite comprehending how Santa was allied with Eaton's, but willing to believe anything if it resulted in a top or truck or a big red fire engine under the tree.

We knew we would receive something for Christmas, but we had a problem. The cause of the worried looks and my little brother's tears was that we had no tree. And Rus was sure that without a tree, there would be no visit from the jolly man in the red suit.

Mama and Papa, Ve and I all tried to reassure him. Sure, there would be a visit from Santa. There would be toys. We wiped his wet eyes and insisted that Santa didn't require a tree. Didn't the children in Holland receive gifts in wooden shoes, and children everywhere get toys and dolls in baskets and stockings?

But Rus continued to weep at intervals. "Why didn't the Indian come?"

In those days, our part of the prairie still bore evidence of the noble tribes who had called that land home. Bare buffalo bones bleached beside the rutted trails, worn by the animals' hoofs as they sought the brown waters of the sloughs or the salt lick or the huge rock that was worn smooth as they rubbed off their heavy winter coats. This land had been Indian land, but we children were only faintly aware of it. In those days we were totally unconcerned that the rightful owners of this miserable terrain had been pushed back from their lands, lands so much better suited to their existence than the pitiful farming that Papa attempted. He had nothing else.

Farther north, maybe thirty miles away, lived a few sad remnants of a band that had once chased the buffalo over the trails, picked the wild strawberries and saskatoons, killed the prairie chickens and rabbits. They had probably enjoyed a much better life than my poor parents, who struggled to somehow wrest a living from this unproductive tract.

We saw the Indian from time to time. He was our friend. He sometimes came by in the summer, driving a malnourished horse hitched to a rattling old wagon, on his way to the cluster of houses on the railroad that we called "town." God knows Bruce was only a dot on the long C.N.R. line, but it was the source of staple groceries and binder twine, new shoes, and everything else we couldn't grow.

The Indian would always stop his anaemic-looking horse by our wire gate and, in a comical pantomime of pulling teats and drinking, ask for milk. Papa always obliged. We didn't have much, but we had lots of milk. The wrinkled brown face would respond with many smiles, and after another pantomime of thanks, the Indian would urge his poor beast to continue the several miles to the tiny hamlet.

Every year now for several years, the Indian had come by a few days before Christmas with a load of evergreen trees to sell in the town. His poor old horse was as miserable as ever and now pulled a set of bobsleighs, piled high with nature's bounty. We had no evergreens of our own, so in return for past favours, he always stopped at our gate and gave us a beautiful fir tree covered with cones and spicy with the delicious odour that to this day means Christmas to me. This tree graced our tiny living room, served as an incentive for Santa to leave lots of gifts, held the tiny twisted wax candles that Mama had ready on the shelf, and received the popcorn strings, cranberry ropes, and paper chains that Ve and I had been making for days.

What had gone wrong? It was three o'clock. Almost time to light the kerosene lamps. Christmas Eve. The Indian hadn't come. And we had no Christmas tree.

As the full extent of the disaster became apparent, my young parents were sick at heart. They had been so sure; he always came. The turkey was ready, the mince pies, the cookies, and the dark fruity cake. The gifts were hidden in the closet, the nuts and the Japanese oranges and the twisted ribbon candies. Tomorrow, unless there was a blizzard, our aunts and uncles would come to dinner, driving their steaming teams over the crusted snow.

But what is Christmas without a tree? The nearest evergreens grew tall and beautiful thirty miles to the north. Papa couldn't hitch up old Cap and Prince and set out now. He would have to go in darkness and maybe face a blizzard, either of which would prevent him from even finding a tree. What to do? As my parents finally put into words the thing we had dreaded to hear, we all set up a howl. There would be no Christmas tree this year!

Unbelievable! My parents looked from one tear-stained face to the other, and Mama began to cry. Papa looked as though he too could shed a tear. It was bad enough to commit these kids to their lonely life on this God-forsaken farm; they surely deserved a tree. Darn that Indian! But he wasn't coming, that was for sure.

We finally cried ourselves out. We would get along without a tree. It wasn't as though Christmas itself was cancelled. We would have all the trappings of the celebration except the tree. But there would be no Christmas smell of pungent evergreen sap, no tiny candles to dimly reveal the presents, no mysterious boughs to hold the little gifts with red ribbon bows, no place for the decorations—no tree! We all howled again, and Mama and Papa repeated again and again that Christmas was coming anyway. It was just going to be a treeless one. Pooh! Forget it. Go to bed. Santa will come, never fear.

Sleep was slow in coming. Mama and Papa were still moving about. We could hear the rustle of heavy brown paper. We hoped that little Rus was already asleep. After all, he still believed that old Santa was coming and, with the amazing faith of a little child, thought that the rotund old fellow could somehow get down our skinny stovepipe. Papa seemed to be bringing something big in from outside. It made a lot of noise. Maybe they had sleds or doll buggies stashed away in the granary. What were they doing out there? Very satisfactory. There certainly were gifts. We lay in the dark and squeezed each other's hands and speculated about our gifts. Who needs a tree? But the odd tear rolled down onto Mama's prized goose-feather pillows before we finally gave up and drifted into dreams.

Christmas morning, dark and pregnant with promise. Bare feet on the icy floor, and a stern command from Papa to stay in bed until he stoked up the heater. Mama echoed his words and added to them: "Children, put on your long underwear. Put on your stockings. Don't come out in your nightgowns! It's too cold!"

That interminable wait. Finally: "Come children. See what Santa brought!"

The living room was dark—except in one corner. Mama was lighting the wax candles. But what were they fastened to? Oh joy! There it stood. A little birch tree as bare as the winter winds had left it. It was festooned with our cranberry ropes, the popcorn, the paper chain, the prized German baubles, the wonderful pastel-coloured candles that cast a soft glow over the presents piled below. It was beautiful! Gorgeous! The nicest tree we ever had!

There have been many lovely trees since that Christmas, beautiful evergreens merging into a composite tree of real charm and grace. But one stands alone in memory—a leafless little birch that a loving father plucked from an Alberta snowbank on Christmas Eve.

11

Our Other Grandpa Pays a Visit

We had been playing a game in Mama's vegetable garden one lovely, warm summer day. We had tired of our stick horses and mudpies and had turned to the rhubarb patch, where we pulled some of the long stalks for parasols. The huge ruffled leaves were perfect protection from the sun, but we soon tired of this, too, and lay in the grass chewing on rhubarb and watching grasshoppers spring from blade to blade, bees sip at the daisies, and a robin in search of his dinner.

Then we hit on a new game, which we called "Rabbits." Down on all fours, we hopped along the neat garden rows methodically gnawing at the tops of the lush little cabbages and cauliflower. One by one, we bit the bright green pointy heads and the delicate white florets. We imagined ourselves to be real rabbits raiding Mama's garden and put in a few extra hops and kicks and squeaks.

We were getting rather full and were beginning to realize that Mama wouldn't be at all pleased with our game when we saw the stranger approaching.

Ve saw him first—a man plodding over the west pasture, carrying a suitcase. Someone we didn't recognize at all. But we knew he must have got off the train in Bruce, otherwise why the suitcase and why on foot?

We stood, all three in a row, staring. Three tanned little prairie kids, two small girls and a smaller boy—bare feet in the warm garden soil, a slight breeze riffling unruly hair and soiled pinafores.

The man waved. We waved back, shading our eyes for a better look. He was getting closer. We didn't know him. We were sure of it. Then a vague memory stirred in Ve's brain. "It's our Other Grandpa!" she shouted, and we all took off for the house to tell Mama that company was coming.

The man with the suitcase was at the gate now. Carefully he opened it, came through, and just as carefully replaced the latch. He put down his suitcase, removed his straw hat, and mopped his brow. Red hair! Now we knew for sure. It was our Other Grandpa. Mama came running out, apron flying, to be folded in a warm hug.

After an excited exchange of greetings and explanations, he turned to us kids.

"Gosh, Myrtle, such lovely children. I should know them, but I'm afraid I don't remember their names. Isn't this biggest girl Vera or Verna or something like that?"

So this was Mama's father—almost a stranger to us. When we spoke of Grandpa, we were always referring to Papa's father, whom we knew fairly well. He had visited the farm a couple of times, and we had visited him in the States just last winter.

Grandpa Sinclair. We may not have known him, but we did know the story. Although Rus was too young to care, Ve and I had talked about it at times. We had also questioned Mama about Lester more than once.

Before we were born, Grandpa's wife, our grandmother, died in childbirth, leaving behind her newborn son. Eighteen-year-old Mama, preparing for her wedding, was suddenly left in charge of a baby, two teenaged brothers, and a ten-year-old sister. Within the year she had a baby of her own, and her hands were very full indeed.

After a while our grandfather remarried and baby Lester and Gladys went to him and his new wife. Auntie Glad was a problem teenager, and poor little Lester embarked on an uneasy childhood where no one really wanted him. Verne and Forrest were on their own by this time.

Grandpa was a restless wanderer who shuttled back and forth from Canada to the States, from the States to Canada. He also embarked on a series of marriages, running the total up to six before his demise. Through all this, his children's lives were always in turmoil. Lester was shuttled from pillar to post, as they say, and periodically Mama had him returned to her if her father was temporarily wife-less.

Grandpa settled in to stay a few days. He unpacked his battered bag with three curious children hovering around. As we had hoped, he had brought candies and some little toys. He was a charming man, and even without the gifts, he would have quickly won our hearts. He took us on his knee, sang songs, told stories, played games, joked, and laughed. He was always smiling and lighthearted. We loved him.

Ve and I were sleeping on the floor so Grandpa could have our bed. But not for long, because the visit was brief. On the second day of this stay, its purpose was revealed. I think Mama guessed it as soon as he came. Since he never wrote to her, she didn't even know he was in the country. There had to be a reason for his visit.

There was.

He wanted to send Lester, now twelve, back to her. The current wife couldn't or wouldn't handle him. Would Myrtle please take him over? What could Mama say but yes? After all, in a way, he was her baby.

When the reason for Grandpa's visit became clear, Papa's attitude toward him cooled a lot. Mama and Papa argued it out in the barn, for privacy, and Papa finally had to give in to Mama's tears and her position that she couldn't turn away her little brother.

So, in a very few days, our Other Grandpa packed his bag and was away. We kids hated to see him go. He was a very charming man, and when Mama saw her cabbages and cauliflower, he talked her out of punishing us. Incidentally, we played "Rabbits" only once.

Almost as speedy as Grandpa's departure was Lester's arrival. A strange man from Vegreville came almost at once with the boy and his few belongings.

Lester was with us for a long time, as it turned out. Papa went to town and bought a couch for him to sleep on in the front room, and Mama set to work washing and mending his threadbare clothes.

"Summer Babes"

So now our uncle was added to the family. Just a little more than a year older than Ve, but our uncle nonetheless. The members of our family reacted to the new arrival each in his own way. Papa hoped he would be some help around the farm. Mama loved him, of course, and tried hard to make up for his unhappy childhood. Ve wasn't pleased; he would now take her place as eldest. He established his relationship with me right away when he called me Fatty. Rus was delighted to have another boy in the family, and he and Lester quickly became pals.

None of us heard anything of our Other Grandpa for years. Sometimes Mama would get a little news from someone else. He was back in the States. He was married again. There were no letters, no Christmas cards, and so far as I know, no money for Lester's needs.

12

Papa Vanquishes a Bogeyman

Ve said she was going home. She picked up her bucket, and I prepared to follow her. Whatever my older sister did, I did too. Lester, looking scared for once, cautioned her that Papa would surely punish us if we didn't finish our job and suggested that we move to the other side of the field.

The slight breeze stirred our hair and blew our thin cotton skirts against our skinny legs. We scuffed our bare feet in the loose dirt of the field as we weighed the consequences of abandoning the task that Papa had set us. Lester picked up his bucket and started off to the far side of the newly-harrowed plot.

We were out to poison gophers. After harrowing the north field, Papa had been very alarmed at the number of gophers running about and had decided to take some action to get rid of the little pests. So he had sent us out, on this breezy day, in an effort to cut down the population before the field was planted. Papa had furnished each of us with an old pail filled with a sloppy wet mash, which was laced with some sort of poison. Along with our bucket went a piece of shingle—Mama couldn't spare any old spoons—and all we had to do was put one scoop of the mixture in every gopher hole we could find.

We hated the gophers because everyone told us we should. Papa said they were a nuisance. The government took an even stronger attitude and paid us—in cash—two cents apiece for gopher tails. We had to agree with wiser heads, but in our secret childish hearts, I think we really liked the lively little brown animals.

For one thing, gophers were always one of the first signs of spring, and we longed for spring after the long cruel winter. When the days grew warm and the crocuses bloomed on Tidy's Hill, they would appear, as sure as the early buttercups. All over the prairie, the cheeky little animals would stand erect at the entrance to their burrows, their shrill whistles piercing the air on all sides. They scurried back and forth, beady eyes bright and watchful, sometimes disappearing into the safety of their underground homes just a whisker ahead of Rover.

But the holes riddled the knolls and fields. Old Buck stepped in them frequently, causing my poor old roan to stumble. In the grain fields, the pesky little rodents did a lot of damage. So we pursued the gophers in a sort of love-hate relationship, drowning them out of their burrows and always eager to add to our frowsy collection of tails.

Papa said it was war, and we were to put out poison. So today, here we were in the north field with our deadly meal for the brown creatures that even now were running all over the place.

We cheated, of course. Some holes got two scoops, as we frequently duplicated our efforts in our lazy way. We looked on our job as a bore, and the sooner we emptied our pails, the sooner we would be finished. Completely ignoring the purpose of the project, we concentrated on getting rid of the poison as soon as possible so we could go home and do something more interesting.

Skirting a small stand of poplar that Papa had left in the field, Ve, always the nervous one, had dropped her shingle in alarm and, whispering loudly to Lester and me, announced that there was someone in the bush.

This wasn't entirely unexpected. Ve had been listening to stories at school lately about bogeymen and strange characters roaming around and had become very fearful of meeting up with someone like that. These nights when we were sent to bed in our unlighted little bedroom, she had taken to pushing me in first, only following when I remained unattacked. I resented being used as a decoy, but so far all had been well. There were no terrors awaiting, and Ve could follow me feeling safe, at least for the night.

We grouped together, eyes riveted on the poplar bush. There was movement there all right, but we could not see very clearly through the leafy growth. It looked something like a man in a black coat. We strained to see his face but couldn't make out any features.

Ve whispered to Lester that he should find out what it could be. Lester hadn't yet achieved his brave period and was as nervous as we were, although he was trying not to show it. As the eldest, and a boy too, he felt compelled to put on a show of courage. He took a few steps toward the bluff, trying for a better look. His bit of shingle was upraised in a gesture that would have been comical if we had been able to see the humour of it. Lester couldn't do much damage to whatever might be lurking behind the poplars with a piece of fragile wood.

The figure in the poplar grove moved slightly from time to time. We stood huddled. Should we run? Perhaps that would aggravate him and he would chase us. How we wished Rover was there, but our dog had gone with Papa and the horses to the south field.

Lester, keeping an eye on the trees, again suggested that we move carefully away. Looking back apprehensively, we saw the black-clad figure stir back and forth, but it did not emerge from the leafy shelter.

The gopher holes on the west side of the field got very hasty attention. Still keeping wary eyes on the poplar bluff and moving ever farther away from it, we deposited our mash quickly; over-dosing, duplicating, and shoving the poison into holes with a speed that we hadn't achieved earlier in the day.

We took the long way home, avoiding the poplars, and from a distance we thought we could see "him" still hiding in the bush.

At the supper table, we sidestepped Papa's questions about how well we had done our job with our story of the mysterious man in the north field. Papa was skeptical, but Mama said he had better investigate.

Papa was tired and had chores to do around the barns, but he brought out Nellie, jumped on her bare back, and rode out to the north field. It was only a short distance, and we were able to watch as he dismounted and strode into the bush. He was out again promptly, carrying something black. It certainly didn't have the substance of a man. Maybe a man's coat?

Papa brought it home on the horse's back so he could reveal the bogeyman to us—a piece of tattered tarpaper that had sailed into the poplar bluff on one of our celebrated Alberta gales.

13

Going to See Auntie

It was strange, though perhaps appropriate, that it happened on Halloween, but it provided a little excitement on a night that would have been like any other on our lonely prairie homestead.

Halloween to us meant a party at school. We spent a lot of time in the days before October 31st drawing jack o'lanterns, witches on broomsticks, ghosts, and black cats. We coloured and cut so that the schoolroom was well decorated for the party, and when the day came, it was a lot of fun. We bobbed for apples and attacked apples on strings, trying to bite them as they swung. We played games and told ghost stories. There were special cookies and cakes.

This party was, of necessity, in the afternoon, and for us, that was it. We didn't know a thing about tricking and treating. Who would we trick anyway? Miles from the nearest neighbour, we couldn't have managed any shenanigans, and we honestly didn't have any idea of dressing up or going from door to door. Papa had a few stories about soaping windows and tipping over backhouses when he was a boy in Illinois, and we listened to these with interest as something that happened long ago and far away.

So after the party at school, we went home to supper and a quiet evening as usual. We didn't even have a pumpkin to carve up, as Papa and Mama didn't grow pumpkins and, for some reason, hadn't encouraged us in that tradition.

It was All Hallows' Eve, and we were grouped around the

coal-oil lamp on the front room table, doing the things we always did. Papa was reading the *Winnipeg Free Press*, Mama was darning socks, Ve and I were playing Rummy, and Rus was down on the floor playing with a top that Papa had made him out of one of Mama's empty sewing spools.

Ve laid down her cards and announced that she had to "go." That meant a trip out back to the shanty with the half-moon cut in the door. We called the little house by several genteel names. We never called it the backhouse! Instead, we said we had to pay a visit down the path or "go see Auntie." Ours was a modest one-holer equipped with old copies of the Eaton's catalogue or, luxury of luxuries, tissue wrappers from a box of apples. In freezing weather, a trip out there was put off as long as humanly possible and then done very quickly indeed!

Anyway Ve had to go, and she wanted me to accompany her. We usually went down the path together at night, but she had just accused me of cheating in the card game so I stubbornly refused.

"Take Rover—he will protect you."

Some of the girls at school had been talking a lot lately about some crazy man that was on the loose, and after the ghost stories at today's party, Ve was even more scared than usual. She was always nervous of bogeymen and badmen. She was still pushing me into the bedroom first, and I was still reporting that all was safe. We would pop into bed very quickly, confident that once the patchwork quilts were pulled over our heads, nothing could harm us.

Poor frightened Ve couldn't wait any longer and stepped out the door, rousing Rover from his cozy nap on the back step. Holding his shaggy ruff in her trusting hand, she set out for "Auntie's."

She was back almost at once, screaming that someone was in the backhouse, holding the door. We knew that none of our family could be there, so that caused quite a commotion. Ve continued to yell, which started Rover barking. Papa and Mama tried to calm her down, but they were puzzled. Papa said that someone going by might have been forced to use our facility, but if so, he must have been on foot because, in the moonlight, there was no sign of a horse or wagon. That didn't make sense anyway—in our world, anyone would have come to the door and said hello and furthermore, there were miles of prairie and bush out there!

Ve was still screaming. Little Rus started to cry. He too had heard of bogeymen. I was stunned, feeling that somehow this was my fault because I had been mean to Ve. Mama had her hands full trying to calm her brood.

Papa said there was only one way to solve this mystery. He refused to believe that there was anyone there who meant any harm. But he did pick up a strong stick on his way past the woodpile. Rover had stopped barking and actually played around Papa's feet on their way down the path. That was a good sign—our dog would have warned of any danger. The rest of us huddled in the lighted doorway, waiting for our father to deal with the intruder.

Papa pounded and pushed hard on the door, but it refused to open. He got angry and demanded that the occupant come out. All was silent within. Rus stopped crying long enough to ask if it was a bear. We were always afraid of bears!

"Come out at once. You are frightening my children. What is going on? Are you sick or something?"

Absolute silence. Not a word. Not a movement. Papa tightened his grip on his stout cudgel, stepped back, and lunged at the flimsy door. Crash! Down it came. No one. Nothing. Just an old broom that had somehow fallen in a way that blocked the door.

Papa said that it was probably some Halloween witch who had to "go" and left her broom behind!

14

The Year Buff Came Down the Chimney

Another Christmas Eve in our lonely prairie home. The weather was much like the year before. It was bitterly cold, and the biting wind blew steadily, assaulting the tiny log cabin in angry gusts. Icicles hung from the eaves like glistening lace curtains. Sometimes, looking out from the tiny windows, we would see one of these icy spears break off and silently stab the drift below.

Papa had shovelled a path to the barns. It was like a deep trench, with sides higher than my head. The dry snow crunched under his boots as, lantern in hand, he came in from feeding the stock. He knocked the snow off his big buckled overshoes, sailed in quickly on a blast of cold air, and hung his mackinaw on a hook inside the door. Blowing out the lantern, he was happy to see his little family awaiting his arrival. The kerosene lamps were lighted, and all were ready to begin the tree-trimming.

No worries about the tree this year. It was already in the front room, bare but lovely, ready to be draped with our decorations. The sharp, clean odour, that fragrance that meant Christmas, drifted all over the house and conjured up all our dreams of gifts and games and gaiety.

The Indian hadn't let us down. He had come quite early, at least two weeks ago, and this time it took two bony old horses to pull his large load of evergreens.

Christmas trees! Our little, brown, wizened friend stopped

his team at our gate and pulled down a beauty for us. With many smiles and gestures, he presented his gift. His English hadn't improved any, but he didn't need words to make us understand. It was a gorgeous fir, plump and green, loaded with cones, and heavily scented with that divine evergreen perfume. Our Christmas tree! We stuck it in a snowbank and danced around it before Papa installed it in the granary. No tears this Christmas. The tree was here!

I think Rus went to the granary every day to reassure himself that the tree was all right. Just the smell in there was enough to set him off wishing for tops and trumpets, drums and dumptrucks. Ve and I just smiled and winked at each other while he chattered on about Santa. We knew something he didn't know, and Mama said we would get a licking if we told him.

We had made our selections early, as soon as the Eaton's catalogue had come in the fall. The thick book had become positively dog-eared as we turned the glossy pages, studying the illustrations, and changing our minds every few days. We hoped that just one of the items would show up under that beautiful tree. Mama made no promises, but we had seen the bulky brown-paper parcels hidden in the bedroom closet.

Now the tree was ready, and so were we. Mama had been busy for weeks baking cookies and cakes and her special mince pies. Just before supper, we had watched her stuff the turkey. Her clever hands just flew as she spooned the dressing into the big bird and trussed him up firmly with lots of string. We laughed as she threaded a big darning needle to sew up the yawning hole at the back. It made us giggle to think of the big fellow, who had fattened in a pen in the barn, being sewed.

Mama tucked the gobbler into her big, black roasting pan, wrapped it in a clean dishtowel, and cautioned us kids to stand back while she opened the trapdoor to the cellar. She carried the turkey down the ladder to keep cool and fresh until tomorrow.

Ve and I had had a busy day and not without frustration. The wind had blown our oat sheaf away. We had read somewhere that, in Sweden, the children put up a bundle of grain for the birds at Yule time. So we had endured cold hands and feet as we walked on top of the drifts to fasten a fat faggot to the clothesline pole, only to see it go sailing away just before darkness fell. We were very upset, but Papa said the birds could get lots of grain around the barn. Provided any birds came out in this weather, he added. It was a nice idea, though, he assured us.

We had finished the supper dishes, putting everything away neatly and with no quarrelling. We hadn't even followed our usual custom of hiding a couple of the more difficult pots in the warming oven. Christmas Eve is no time to cheat! Now all was ready. Mama stood on a chair in her bedroom to get the precious ornaments from the top of the cupboard. The waxy twisted candles in their little box came next, all pink and blue and green and yellow, with the funny clips to fasten them to the branches. We sniffed their waxy odour. They too smelled like Christmas.

We girls brought our decorations from under our bed. We had enough for several trees—popcorn strings, cranberry ropes, red and green paper chains. This year we had tried something new: popcorn balls. In spite of blistered fingers and sticky clothes, only six had turned out perfectly, but they were ready, with coloured ribbons for hanging, and sitting in a shoebox.

When all the garlands and baubles were on, Papa held Rus up to put the star on top. How beautiful it was! The glittering ornaments caught the light from the candles, reflecting it back to the tinsel strands. There were mysterious shadows under the boughs where we hoped that gifts would be hidden in the morning. Surely no one anywhere had a lovelier tree!

Old Buff admired the tree too and moved in to amuse himself by batting around a glass angel within his reach. We weren't going to let him ruin our decorations, so Mama gave him a swat, and he disappeared fast.

When Rus was ready for bed, he couldn't find the cat. He was accustomed to having Buff sleep at the foot of his crib and tearfully announced that he couldn't sleep without him. We all joined in the search, but even with all the hunting and calling "kitty, kitty," Buff did not show himself. He must have been very humiliated when Mama slapped him. Papa got really cross, but he convinced Rus that our yellow pet would come sneaking out when all was quiet. Rus finally stopped crying, carefully hung his stocking on a chair by the heater, and went to bed. He was soon asleep.

Ve and I hung our stockings too, performing a Yuletide ritual that we would practise for many years to come. When we went to bed, there was still no sign of the cat. Papa opened the door to have a look at the weather. The wind had died down. It was as cold as ever, but now the big yellow moon was drifting in a star-studded sky. "Perfect for Santa's ride," laughed Papa as he blew out the lamp.

We had a hard time falling asleep. The moon shone brightly into our bedroom window, and we chattered on about tomorrow's joys until Papa called from their bedroom that we had better get to sleep, fast. After that we continued on, in whispers under the quilts, until we drifted away.

It seemed only moments later that there was a tremendous crash. This was followed immediately by our four-year-old brother running out in his sleepers, yelling at the top of his lungs.

"It's Santa! Santa's come!"

Rus was followed by a confused Papa in his long underwear and by Mama in her flannelette nightgown. We girls rushed out too. We knew there was no Santa. At least we thought we knew. But somebody had come; something had made a big noise to break the peace of the silent night. Had the jolly old fellow really tried to come down our stovepipe and maybe knocked it down?

The pure moonlight revealed the cause of the commotion even before Mama could light the lamp.

Our lovely tree lay on its side on the front-room floor amid broken baubles and scattered garlands. Some of the candles were broken. The tinsel still clung to the branches in confused loops. A red truck had been activated by the fall and rested against the leg of the table. Various tissue-wrapped parcels lay here and there. Two Eaton's beauties lay on their backs, staring up at us in wide-eyed astonishment.

While we were all righting the tree, it was easy to figure out what had happened. Old Buff had come out of his hiding place and, in the bright peace of the moonlight, decided to play with the tantalizing ornaments in undisturbed enjoyment. Somehow he had pulled the tree down. Once more he was nowhere to be found.

For years after, we referred to that Christmas as the one when Buff came down the chimney.

15

A Berry Bonanza

We set out early. The running boards of the 490 Chev were lashed so high with bundles that we could hardly get in the car. There were two washboilers to bring the berries home in, lard pails, rolls of bedding—everything we would need for camping out.

The pails and other buckets were full of food for our meals, but we fully expected them to come back filled with saskatoons, raspberries, gooseberries, and whatever else we could pick on the big island.

Some of the neighbours reported that the berry crop was very good this year, and when Mama heard that, she decided we would all go and stock up for the winter.

Mama was an ardent berry-picker. My earliest memories contain glimpses of her surrounded by tall grass and mosquitoes, patiently filling a dishpan with the biggest, juiciest wild strawberries I have ever seen. Since the sort of weather that produces an excellent strawberry crop also produces a hearty insect population, the bites had to be endured. Nothing could keep our mother from the berry patch. She would build a smudge in an old pail and pick on.

The big island was in Birch Lake, and that was thirty or forty miles away from the farm. We had the Chev now, and it could be done. If it rained, we would have a hard time because the prairie roads turned to greasy gumbo in wet weather. If this happened, the car could slide into the ditch or become hopelessly mired in some mudhole. But the weather looked good, and our hopes and spirits were high as Papa cranked up the car and we all piled in.

We kids were excited at several prospects. First of all, the lake. We had never seen a body of water larger than John Theaker's big slough, and Birch Lake was said to be enormous! Water as far as the eye could see! That seemed incomprehensible to children who were used to endless prairie. We had never slept under the stars either, and that seemed like high adventure until Rus nervously asked about bears.

Papa assured us there were no bears in that part of the country and that the big island probably had no animals at all. We looked forward to spreading our blankets under a big tree and falling asleep to the soft song of the waves rolling into the shore.

In a few places, the road was graded and barbed-wire fences marked boundaries. Sometimes we travelled over two rutted tracks across the open prairie. At noon, we spread our lunch beside the road, and the fried chicken disappeared quickly, for we were anxious to get to the lake.

Rolling along after lunch, we noticed that the landscape began to change. There were more hills—not large, but more than at home. The road became quite sandy, and the wildflowers were different and of greater variety. Wild roses pressed right up to the car. Never before had we seen the wild bergamot that bloomed on the hillsides, purple against the background of silver willow. There were tiger lilies, brown-eyed susans, fireweed, Indian paintbrush, and blazing star, dark red and beautiful. On our stops we had a chance to inspect the smaller flowers half-hidden in the grass: shooting stars, Indian tobacco, prairie aster, and wild onion. Alberta is blessed with hundreds of varieties of wildflowers, and we revelled in this colourful floral tapestry that Nature had unrolled for us.

We passed a few other homesteads, much like ours, with modest farmhouses, barns, windmills, and cattle pens. Women hoeing in their gardens waved a greeting. More than once we had to stop and shoo a herd of somnolent cows off the road. Shy, strange kids, bareback on skittish ponies, pulled on the reins as our car passed them. Sometimes we watched another traveller approach. Farmers in wagons or buggies, on their way to town or a neighbouring farm, stopped for a chat about the weather or the crops. We met several cars, too, loaded with families much like ours, off on some errand in the other direction.

The sun was getting low in the sky when, after a long, laboured climb, the Chev topped a larger hill and below us we saw the lake!

To our eyes, it was as big as an ocean. There it lay, with real waves rolling in the sun; big and blue and even vaster than we had imagined.

And right over there was the big island, covered with heavy timber and about ten times as large as we had thought it would be!

Down the hill, through several wire gates (carefully closed behind us), and we were there.

The island was hardly an island. It was separated from the mainland by a very narrow, very shallow channel. With our bundles on our heads and the car left behind on the bank, we waded across to our campground. Papa built a fire, Mama began to set out food, and we kids scrambled from bush to bush, filling our mouths with the biggest, reddest raspberries we had ever seen.

It was a berry bonanza. All the next day, we picked until our lard pails overflowed into the kettles, which in turn overflowed into the washboilers. We wandered from one end of the island to the other, sometimes meeting other families.

We got lost and reunited with each other after much yoo-hooing back and forth. We were enchanted by the tall trees, the hawks screaming overhead, and the azure expanse of the lake when we looked out from the shore. Mama did not have to urge us on in our picking. Our mouths and pails were full most of the time.

On the third day, it was time to start home. Every pot and pan was filled with berries, and yet all over the place, the bushes were loaded as though none had been picked.

Mama was ecstatic. There were gallons of saskatoons, ripe brown gooseberries, pincherries, chokecherries, wild cranberries, raspberries—full of the delicious promise of jams and jellies, preserves, and juicy pies. We had picked quarts and quarts of summer's bounty, to be spooned from Mama's mason jars when the winter winds blew and summer was only a memory.

The drive home was uneventful, unless one counted two flat tires. This common mishap was accepted in the usual way. Papa got out his kit of tire patches and mended the offending inner tube while we kids explored the fields and bushes around. When the patch seemed to have taken, Papa pumped up the skinny rubber tube, forced it back into the narrow tire, tightened the nuts and bolts around the rim, and we were away again. Two flats were pretty good for such a long trip.

Some busy days followed, with the preserving kettle bubbling away on the hot stove and rows and rows of jelly jars shining like clear red jewels as they cooled on the kitchen table.

The trip to Birch Lake became an annual affair, and it never lost its enchantment. You might say that was our summer holiday.

16

The School Fair

When Ve was older, she used to bring out a blue card sometimes at parties or other fun times that announced her as winner of first prize for "Oddest Shape." Actually, Ve had a nice shape when she grew up, and the card hadn't anything to do with her figure. She got it at the school fair for a carrot that was so twisted and contorted, it looked like a deformed starfish.

The annual school fair was a big event for us. It was held in August, in Viking, and was the culmination of many weeks of preparation.

We left for town early. Our excitement grew as we neared the little village. We could see many other families on the road, and we waved to friends and strangers alike as we all converged on the fair grounds.

Nearly everyone had the same plan as us—to get there well ahead of parade time and decorate the car in town. All that crepe paper would surely have blown off on the bumpy road.

We stopped at a little bluff north of town and got busy with the job of making the Chev look really festive. Red, white, and blue ribbons threaded through the wheel spokes and big sheaves of ripe wheat and oats, tied with red ribbon and placed on either side of the windshield, soon began to transform the car. All around the body, big bands of red, white, and blue streamers were stretched from the roof of the car to the headlights. We had flowers from home and a few early coloured leaves. We fastened them here and there on the running boards and bumpers. When we were finished, we were sure that our entry would win some sort of prize.

We were all dressed up for the occasion, too. Ve and I wore dresses of pongee silk and straw hats with ribbon streamers down the back and tiny flower sprigs on the ribbon. We had long white stockings and white shoes. Mama wore her best navy blue dress and a hat to match. Rus sported short pants and a beanie cap, while Papa was in a suit and wore a white shirt, a big change from the overalls and work shirts he wore around the farm most days. Papa had his new cap on, too, and tilted it at a jaunty angle as we drove past the creamery and Barker's coal and wood yard on our way to the schoolgrounds.

A lot of vehicles were there before us, all ready for the parade. There were cars and trucks as well as hayracks, buggies, tractors, lumber wagons, and dray wagons, and they were decorated with grain and flowers, flags and bunting, crepe-paper streamers and vegetables. Restless horses switched at flies and nervously eyed the passing cars. Everyone watched the man with the megaphone on the platform in front of the town school, waiting for him to announce the parade.

Round and round went the gay rigs. Up Main Street (that was only two blocks), past the curling rink, past the town pump and the Catholic church, and, of course, past the judges' stand on the edge of the schoolgrounds. Decisions were finally made, and the honoured vehicles proudly displayed their blue ribbons; our Chev didn't win a prize.

As soon as the parade broke up, we were away to begin the fun of the fair. We soon found the booth where we could buy treats and carefully untied our knotted handkerchiefs to get one of our precious little nickels. The ice cream soon dripped from the end of the soft cone, and we had to lick both ends to get it all. Little Rus had a shinplaster to spend, and we older sisters watched carefully to be sure he didn't lose his change.

The sports program was well underway. There was a ball game behind the school, a basketball game on the schoolgrounds, and a full slate of races in front of the grandstand. Foot races and sack races, along with potato and egg-and-spoon relays, followed one another, while harassed officials ran about trying to keep toddlers and dogs off the track.

Parents were kept busy rounding up their kids to have a quiet picnic lunch in the shade behind the school or under a tree.

Somehow we found time to go into the school and look at the exhibits. How big this school was! It had four large rooms, and we walked respectfully through the quiet halls and up the wide stairs. Here were our maps, handwriting samples, and watercolour landscapes. How we had laboured over these! Mrs. Bender had made us do them over and over until they were as perfect as we could make them.

All the things we had prepared were displayed, as well as entries from dozens of other schools. Here were all the vegetables we had weeded and watered, the collections of leaves and flowers, the butterfly collection that the whole school had made. Our baking was neatly placed on paper plates, with small slices cut away where the judges had sampled. And here were the sewing entries: the neatly hemmed dishtowels, the dusting mitts, the teacloths with embroidered corners. The rule book had specified a sample of a darned sock and a plain patch; there were lots of entries in those classes. The competition for the best thrift project, a garment made from a bleached flour sack, was one of the largest. Everyone was making clothes from flour bags in those days.

Our teacher, Mrs. Bender, was delighted to see that our school had won more than its share of prizes. We would have lots of the coloured prize cards to display when we went back in September. There were also the modest cash prizes to look forward to.

The fair was nearly over. Our clothes were dirty; our nickels were spent. Rus had fallen in a race and skinned his knee. We were all tired and slightly sick from overeating. Papa had to get back to the farm to feed the stock and milk the cows. It was a wonderful day, and we would all look forward to next year and another school fair.

17

Prairie Fire!

Lester climbed up the ladder on the windmill, almost to the platform on the top. He yelled down to Mama that, indeed, it was a prairie fire, and it was burning on the other side of the knoll. We three younger ones climbed up behind him to get a better look. Sure enough, there was smoke rising, and we could see the flames at the edge moving before our eyes, steadily eating at the dry grass on the other side of the rise that we called Tidy's Hill. The wind was from the southwest, so the fire was moving away from our place, and we knew it would not threaten us unless the wind changed.

Almost at once, Papa rode up on Nellie. He had been in the south field mending the fence, and he called quickly to Lester to put the pony away and help him harness the team and hitch it to the wagon. Mama ran to the granary and began to pile empty gunny sacks by the door. Papa drove the wagon beside the water trough and loaded on several empty barrels. Everybody helped fill them with water, and Papa threw on the sacks. He kept urging everyone to hurry, and we ran for more pails and bags. When the barrels were full, Papa told Lester to drive the wagon and get going.

Lester drove off with the barrels slopping, pounding the reins on the horses' rumps to urge them to greater speed.

Now Papa brought out Cap and Prince and hitched them to the plough. While he fastened the traces and adjusted the harness with expert speed, Hans Otto, from the farm to the south, went by with his team and wagon; he too was loaded with barrels. Right behind him came Joe de Rosiers in his democrat, and he pulled into our place to fill some tubs and cans at our well.

From our place on the ladder, which we had resumed as soon as Lester and Papa had disappeared over the hill, we could see the farmers from all around converging on the fire, beating its edges with wet sacks. Some of the rigs were driving back and forth from the slough, where other men were standing hip-deep in the brown water, filling more and more barrels. The ploughs continued moving out of sight, and we knew that the men were going on ahead to make a fireguard to stop the fire with a line of freshly-ploughed furrows.

The flames moved swiftly and steadily northeast, and soon we gave up our places on the windmill. We could no longer see the teams and the men. The air was filled with a pale blue smoke, and the acrid smell of burning grass hung over everything. The land to the north stretched away, black now, with a poplar bluff here and there still burning and smoke rising from tufts of vegetation.

It was one of the first warm days of spring, and we had been very busy cleaning up the yard. We had raked up all the dead grass from last year, picked up all the trash around the caragana hedge, and collected all the little sticks that winter winds had left behind. Mama had been well pleased with our efforts as we gathered the rakings into neat piles and carried the rubbish to a spot over in the corner of the yard to make a big pile for burning. Even little Rus had hauled with his wagon, picking up broken glass and bones that Rover had left behind. Mama finally pronounced her satisfaction with the job, and told Lester that he could set a match to the heap of trash and burn it. That fire had been very pleasant to watch; a prairie fire, uncontrolled and racing across the open plain, was another thing—dangerous and fearful.

After the bonfire was spent, Mama had Lester hitch Buck to the stoneboat and haul the dead ashes away, over the hill. The yard looked clean and tidy. We had done a good morning's work and had been sitting on the stoop having lemonade and cookies when we had noticed the smoke rising.

A prairie fire is not as spectacular as a forest fire, but it can

"Field"
1989

strike fear into the hearts of those who live on the open plains. Even we kids knew that until the men out there could stop its steady advance, it would burn up stacks of hay, granaries, fences, even houses and barns. We thought of all the little nests that the ducks were building in the willows by the slough and the prairie chickens in the long grass.

Nearly everyone had a fireguard ploughed around his house, but unless the fire was checked, everything in its path would burn.

About sunset, Lester came home with the team and wagon. He was able to report that the men had put the fire out, or nearly out, but that they would watch it through the night. In answer to Mama's questions, he was able to tell us that there were over twenty men fighting the blaze, that the farmers' wives up north were feeding them, and that the fire had burned eighteen miles before it was brought under control. Some haystacks and the old abandoned house on the Riley place had been burned, as well as the cattle chutes down by the coulee, where the livestock had been driven for dipping last fall.

Papa came home very late, when we kids were in bed.

The next day we found out how the fire had started.

It wasn't the sun shining on a piece of broken glass, as we had speculated, nor some careless smoker dropping a match in the dry grass. Remember those ashes that Lester had hauled away from our yard? They were not as cold and lifeless as we had thought. The blackened prairie led away from the exact spot where Lester had dumped the remains of our bonfire.

18

Daisy, Daisy

It wasn't anything new, Lester throwing me out of the buggy on the way home from school. It happened once a week or so. He was always pitching me out on the prairie, throwing my lunch pail after me, and forcing me to walk home the rest of the way. My pail was so dented and banged up that the letters spelling out "Swift's Silverleaf Lard" were all distorted, and Mama could hardly force the lid on when she packed my lunch.

No use complaining to Papa. He reminded me that Lester was older, and he was responsible for driving old Buck and getting us safely to school and back. Ve wasn't much help either. She didn't seem to irritate Lester like I did and stayed neutral in most of our arguments.

Lester and I were natural enemies, and I always seemed to get the worst of it. This time we were hardly a mile from the schoolhouse when he turned in his seat and pushed me from my perch on the rear box. Next thing I knew, I was on the dusty road, and my pail came clanking down in front of me. If I had been quick enough, I could have run and clung to the back of the buggy, as I had done lots of times before, but old Buck sprang to a trot, and our vehicle, with Ve and Lester laughing and yelling, disappeared quickly into the distance.

Tears of rage coursed down my cheeks, and knowing that I had provoked the incident this time didn't help at all. In our one-room school, there were no secrets, and all the pupils participated, more or less, in all the classes. I had listened with interest and smug satisfaction when Mrs. Bender scolded Lester in class that day. Lester was in grade eight; I was only in grade five and assigned to some busy work on the other side of the room. But every child in the schoolroom had heard the teacher reprimand Lester.

We hadn't got very far on the ride home when I reminded Lester of his humiliation. As a result, here I was on the prairie, and I was going to have to walk alone past the haunted house. I was scared witless!

We had become increasingly nervous going back and forth past this scary building every day. The stories we told each other had become more and more elaborate as we gave full rein to our childish imaginations. We had done it to ourselves. Now we were afraid to pass it, even in daylight.

It wasn't a bit like the haunted houses in storybooks. In the first place, it wasn't even a real house. It was more of a shack. It sat back a little way from the road, in a skimpy poplar grove. It had been empty now for several years, and time and neglect had taken their toll. The tiny windows had lost most of their glass panes, and the one door swung in the wind. The outside had never been painted; the walls, which had been bright new lumber once, had turned to dull grey. The privy out back reflected the state of the shanty, its open door sagging on a lone hinge. Our vivid imaginations had it inhabited with bats.

It hadn't been much when old Mose lived there; now it was sad and forlorn. We chose to think it haunted because one cold winter morning, Joe de Rosiers had found Mose and his dog frozen to death, huddled on the cheerless iron cot in the frigid room. Papa said they must have been dead at least a week, ever since the forty-five below night when Old Mose had somehow stumbled home, too dead drunk to make a fire in the cast-iron stove or even to close the door. In that frigid room, he and his rheumatic old dog had perished from the cold.

Around this simple and tragic story, we had built up all our tales of a poor spectre that wandered endlessly, followed by a ghost dog limping painfully on crippled feet, the two of them eternally seeking a warm fire and peace at last. As we drove by in our buggy on the way to school, we expected to see the poor old bachelor come creeping on frozen legs from the gaping door, or even from the poplar grove. He would be ghostly white, covered with thick rime, eternally gelid.

This was the first time I had been kicked out on the far side of the haunted house. As soon as I saw Lester urge old Buck into a quick trot and clatter down the twin ruts leading to home and safety, I knew that for the first time, I would have to pass it alone and on foot.

Clutching my lunch pail, I set out resolutely. I would have to do it.

A bend in the road and Old Mose's abandoned homestead appeared in view. My bare feet quickened their pace. My heart pounded, my mouth was dry, my eyes were fixed solidly on the derelict shack. Somehow my reluctant legs would have to carry me past the haunted house, fast. That was it: make a run for it, get it over with quickly.

Suddenly, I stopped in my tracks. There was movement in the shack. Something white had moved past the tiny window. I was rigid. The pounding of my heart had increased until it seemed to shake my whole body. My fingers dripped moisture on the tin pail that I pressed to my chest. Screaming was impossible. My legs were as stiff and unresponsive as two boards.

Paralyzed with fear, my gaze still riveted on the tumbledown hovel, I waited for the ghost. This was the climax of all our stories—this was the end! Old Mose had found a victim; he was coming to me to plead for deliverance from his unhappy state. What could I do?

Well, I couldn't run. I was an immovable ten-year-old statue, firmly stuck to the prairie trail, rigid and frozen with terror. My eyes never left the shack. The ghost was coming, and there was no escape!

I was a farm child. I knew a cow when I saw one. The ghost lumbered awkwardly through the narrow doorway, miraculously metamorphosing into our pet white milk cow, Daisy.

When I finally got home, Lester was slopping the pigs, Ve was setting the table for supper, and Mama was hailing me from the kitchen door. I unfastened the barbed-wire gate, herded Daisy in with a final slap of my willow switch, and carefully placed the wire loop over the gatepost. I felt grown-up and competent. Papa was very pleased that I had found our stray cow. He had been out on the prairie all morning looking for her without success.

That wasn't the last time I got thrown out of the buggy. But, somehow, the scary tales about the haunted house had lost their power to frighten me. I was inclined to giggle a bit when we passed the crumbling shack.

I never told anyone until now where I found Daisy.

19

The Christmas Concert

The excitement had been building for weeks; on the day of the concert, it was almost too much for us children to bear.

We spent the entire morning on the dress rehearsal. We went right through the program, and at last, Mrs. Bender was satisfied. There was a lot of last-minute instruction on details. The older children were to help the little ones to dress. Performers were to sit in the front row and were not to go backstage until called. "Do not start singing until Mrs. Finnemore gives the signal," etc., etc. Our teacher had a reputation for putting on excellent concerts and hoped this would be the best ever.

At noon we were all dismissed so that the school could be prepared for the evening. When we returned in the late afternoon, we couldn't believe our eyes. The room had been transformed! It was wondrous! There were decorations everywhere. Red and green crepe-paper streamers sprang from the four corners of the ceiling, twisting and meeting in the centre at a big red bell. There were red bows on the windows and loops of green rope in between. Our Christmas artwork hung on the walls. The lamps were lit. Everything looked so different now—like fairyland or some magic place.

And the tree! We stood and gazed, entranced. It had gone up in the afternoon, too, and it was lovely, heavily draped with silver tinsel, paper chains, popcorn and cranberry garlands, and tiny pastel candles. The presents were piled underneath, neatly wrapped in white tissue paper, decorated with

Christmas seals, and tagged with the children's names. There would be a gift for every child in the district, from the tiniest baby to the eldest pupil in the school. Mrs. Bender, like Santa, had made a list and checked it twice.

A crew of fathers had put up the stage. Tiny as it was, it still left very little room for the audience and the tree. The only dressing rooms were the small pits at the sides, one of which was further eroded by the organ, so the donning of costumes would be a hasty affair, with little room to manoeuvre. Bedsheets were strung on a clothesline to serve as curtains.

As each child arrived in the room, something almost magical seemed to happen. Like the schoolroom, we too were changed. We were not ordinary at all now; we were performers, ready to go on that stage and delight the audience that was gathering out in front.

This was unmistakably the social event of the season. Everyone was there, and we were filled with confidence. We could do it. Our parents and our teacher would be very proud of us tonight.

Just before the curtains parted, Mrs. Bender whispered to some of us that Mac McLeod was in the audience. He was the teacher at Woodside, the neighbouring school. He too was proud of his concerts, so now we had an additional challenge. We must do better than Woodside!

The lamps and candles shed a soft glow on the expectant faces watching the stage. Mrs. Finnemore took her place at the organ, and the curtains were pulled back to reveal the opening number.

The programme was traditional and predictable. There were the usual medley of carols, the recitations, the play, the tableaux, the monologue, and the grand finale with the whole school holding up the cardboard letters spelling out MERRY CHRISTMAS. It progressed to the end with a few delays, some stage fright, and in one case, a downright refusal to perform.

For weeks we had been coaching Rus to make his stage debut with a simple little recitation:

"When I was a little boy, just so high,"
(Show them how high, Rus.)
"Mama used to spank me, and make me cry."
"Now I'm a BIG boy, and Mama can't do it,"
(Reach way up, Rus.)
"So Daddy takes a big stick and hops right to it!"

Rus was perfect in his lines at home. Would we ever be proud of him!

When his turn came, our little brother mounted the stage confidently. Mama and Papa beamed encouragement from the audience. But at the second line, Rus lost his nerve and ran off the stage into Mama's arms, absolutely refusing to continue.

Our audience was uncritical, and we got lots of applause. Even when Edna muffed her line a bit and spoke of "jumping out of *bread* on a cold morning," it was only the rest of the cast who giggled.

After the final number, props and costumes were hastily discarded, and it was time for the tree and Santa Claus. A loud clanging of sleigh bells outside signalled his arrival. His ho-ho-ho's had a decided Scandinavian accent. A quick check of the audience confirmed the suspicions of the older children that it was Ole Hanson in the ill-fitting red suit. But the little kids were entranced as he made his way to the tree and began to give out the packages.

As well as a tissue-wrapped gift, each child got a leno bag filled with an orange, an apple, nuts, ribbon candies, and other assorted sweets.

Mothers kept a nervous eye on the tree as the room erupted with a sea of tissue paper and assorted wrappings. Then, a few families bundled their children into their coats and overshoes for the chilly trip home, but most stayed for the dancing. The stage was quickly dismantled, the tree carried outside. The musicians got out their instruments, and the floor was swept and sprinkled with powder.

The concert was over. Now it was time for the grownups to celebrate the Christmas season.

20

Prairie Bears

Our encounter with the bear was really Lester's fault, just one more thing that we had against him.

We had never seen a bear. Coyotes skulked across the prairie, and once we saw a lynx, but never a bear. Everyone said there were no bears in our part of Alberta, and that was okay with us. Bears were fine in picture books and suitable for intimidating Rus, but we didn't want to meet one.

In the year of the bear, Lester had become insufferable. He was growing up fast, becoming strong and muscular, and his head was swelling faster than the rest of him. Ve, Rus, and I had to listen to a lot of bragging and blowing about his strength, his bravery, and his skills. We were sick of it. He was forever showing off his biceps to our little brother and laughing at the marble-sized lump on Rus's arm. Ve and I watched in silent fury. We were girls and didn't have to have muscles. We just wished that Lester would go away again.

He was doing a lot of bragging at Haeberle's place, too. Whenever Papa sent Lester to help our neighbour with the haying or fence-building, Charlie Haeberle got a lot of this hot air coming his way. Lester, according to himself, was the strongest, bravest thing around. He was afraid of nothing. He could whip anyone. He could lift and pull and push. And if he ever met a lion or a tiger or a bear, well, it could look out!

I guess Papa was sort of relieved when Lester went to help Charlie so he didn't have to listen to him day after day. Lester was glad to go to Haeberles' because Zelda was fourteen now and he was beginning to notice girls. Mr. Haeberle was trying to keep him away from his pretty daughter, but Lester was showing up on their doorstep pretty regularly.

We were always glad when our uncle was away from the farm. Not that we ever called him uncle. We called him some other things, mostly behind his back, but never uncle. With him out of the way, we could play our kid games in peace, and no one would make fun of us or call us babies.

It was on a summer evening, warm and peaceful, quiet and lonely as only a night on the prairie can be, that we saw the bear. The dust lay thick on the half-mile of road to Haeberles' farmhouse. Our bare feet made no sound as we moved along in the dark, looking at the brilliant stars in the velvet sky.

We were happy. Mama had let us go out alone, a thing we were never allowed to do at night unless Lester went with us. But Lester had saddled old Buck to ride over to Olsens' for the mail. After we had begged and begged, Mama finally said we could walk up and visit with the Haeberle kids for just one hour.

That put Ve in charge of us two younger ones, and we arranged ourselves accordingly. One on each side of her, we meandered along looking for the Big Dipper, the Little Dipper, and the other constellations Papa had pointed out to us.

With our heads in the stars, at first we didn't notice the bulky dark thing that crept out of the deep roadside ditch. It gave a couple of low, throaty growls. We froze. Then we gave way to terror. The still prairie air was lacerated with our screams and sobs.

Ve, poor girl, couldn't scream. We younger ones nearly choked her as we clung to her. We were wrapped tightly around her, screaming, yelling, wailing. We couldn't look at the bear. We clung in a tight knot in the middle of the road and waited for our doom. It touched us! Help! Save us! Oh, Mama! Oh, Papa! Oh, God!

For a moment we weren't aware that we were saved. We felt no tearing of cruel black claws, but a hand on our shoulders. Someone spoke.

It was Charlie Haeberle, come to rescue us! Out of the darkness loomed our neighbour—big strong Charlie—

soothing, reassuring. We were saved. He had frightened the bear away.

Gradually our sobs subsided. Three frightened youngsters all talked at once, telling about the bear. "Oh, thank you, Mr. Haeberle. Thanks for coming along. You frightened it away. Thank you. Thank you. No bear would attack with you here."

He finally calmed us down. He had been coming to our place to return Papa's crowbar. No, he didn't see any bear. Guess it wouldn't bother a big man, especially one with a crowbar in his hand. "Don't cry, kids, you're safe. I'll take you home now."

Somehow the big man got his arms around three white-faced kids and a crowbar, and, still in a tight little group, we moved along to the haven of our little home. The yellow lamplight shining softly through the kitchen window never looked more inviting, more comforting, more safe.

When Mama opened the door, she nearly fainted when she saw three little ones with tear-streaked faces and terror-filled eyes. Ve's dress was torn to ribbons from our panicky clawing. Behind this sad trio stood our neighbour, looking as big and solid as a saviour should.

Again, we all talked at once. Mama and Papa were incredulous. A bear? But we knew. We saw it. Mr. Haeberle hadn't seen him, but we had. He had saved us.

Papa said there weren't any bears. Mama said maybe it was a stray calf or a pig or something like that. But we saw it. It was a bear. It was all humpy; it was black; it came right at us. If Mr. Haeberle hadn't come along, you wouldn't have seen us alive again. We all cried once more.

Finally we quieted down. Mama told us to get washed and go to bed. That was enough for one night. She shouldn't have let us go out alone. That was the last time. If we said we had seen a bear, well, maybe we had, but he was long gone by now.

Our rescuer got many hugs and kisses before we went to our beds. And when we said our prayers, God must have been astounded at the blessings sought for one Alberta farmer.

Ve and I had hardly got settled in bed when I felt thirsty. As I opened the door to go to the kitchen, I heard a snatch of a strange conversation from the grownups in the front room. Charlie Haeberle was speaking.

"Well, John, now that the kids are in bed, I'll try to explain something. You aren't going to like it, John, or you, Myrtle, but I can't go home, or even look you two in the face again, unless I confess.

"What happened out there is all my fault. I'll try to explain, and please try to understand."

Mama and Papa must have stared in astonishment. Ve and I couldn't see their faces, concealed as we were at the half-opened bedroom door. But we didn't miss a word.

"Well, John and Myrtle, here it is. You know Lester and his ever-lasting bragging." Ve and I nudged each other. "When I heard someone coming down the road in the dark, I didn't realize it was three little kids. They weren't talking; I just knew someone was coming. So help me I thought it was Lester.

"I'm their bear. I scrunched down in the ditch and I growled. I wanted to play a trick on Lester. I wouldn't have scared your three for anything. It was stupid of me, and now I'm too ashamed to explain to them. They think I saved their lives, and they are going to hate me when they learn the truth.

"They are going to hate me, and I'm really fond of them. But they will see bears in every bush from now on, and they have to know. Please tell them in the morning. Maybe they will understand and forgive me. I'm going home now. I'm really very sorry. Thanks for the loan of your crowbar."

As usual, Rus was up very early the next morning, and Lester heard all about the bear before breakfast. At the table, between generous spoonfuls of porridge, he went on about how he would have dealt with the bear. That animal would have been reduced to bear steaks so fast; he would have turned him inside out; we would have a new bear rug today; we kids should never go out without him; and so on.

Ve and I could see the funny side of it by now, and we giggled and carried on until Papa told us to shut up and eat our breakfast. Rus was understandably puzzled. After breakfast Mama and Papa told us what we already knew. Rus was relieved that there were no bears around the farm, and we were all pretty mad at Mr. Haeberle for a while.

But the Haeberle kids got some new cylinder records for their Edison, and we didn't have a gramophone, so we were soon making regular trips up the road again, but only in daylight.

Lester had discovered that the Olsens' Karen was a very attractive girl, much prettier than Zelda, so he was over at their place a lot. Soon Oscar Olsen was hearing plenty of Lester and asking Papa to keep him at home. Please.

We never saw another bear as long as we lived on the farm.

There are no bears in that part of Alberta.

21

A Lousy Experience

"Stop scratching your head and eat your supper. It isn't nice to do that at the table."

"But Mama, my hair itches and itches."

"Maybe you should comb it. It's all messy." That was Ve.

"I did comb it, but it's still so itchy." I dug away at my scalp.

Mama put down her fork and got up from the table. She walked around to my place and stood over me. Then she bent and looked along the part in my blonde curls. I couldn't see her face, but heard her exclamation—a mixture of surprise and disgust.

"My child, your head is crawling with lice!"

"Lice—ugh." That was Ve again. "I'm not sitting beside you. They're catching!"

She picked up her plate and moved to the other side of the table beside Rus, who was asking, "What is lice?" and getting no answer at all. Papa kept on with his meat and potatoes as though his daughter had lice in her hair every day.

Now Mama started scolding. "I told you not to hang your coat on a hook with other children's at school. I said to pick a separate one."

"But Mama, there aren't enough hooks. I do hang my coat on an empty hook, and then someone hangs his toque and scarf and everything on top of mine."

"Well," said Mama, "this has to be dealt with at once."

We were spending the winter in Vegreville. We were there for the same old reason—money. The crop had been poor, as usual, and someone had found Papa a job in the lumberyard. Leaving the livestock in the care of Uncle Forrest and Aunt Hilda, we moved to the town north of us for the winter so Papa could earn some badly-needed dollars selling lumber and nails.

We had a pretty good time in Vegreville and a few mild adventures. Ve and I went to school. I don't remember my teacher's name or the names of my classmates, except for one or two. I guess the incident with the lice is about all that stays in my mind about grade six in that town.

I do remember one pal though—a handsome, blue-eyed blonde boy. He was, undeniably, my first boyfriend, or beau as it would have been called then, but he was also my best friend in Vegreville. I never thought of him as a boyfriend; maybe he had a crush on me. He and I played together after school, hooking our sleds on to the back of farmers' sleighs as they moved up the snowy main street and getting a free ride to the edge of town, then waiting for another rig to take us back.

His name was Robly Comes. Nearly every day he brought me a small gift scrounged from home—a few crayons, an orange, the prize from a box of Cracker Jack. Ve teased me about him. She called him "Wobbly Combs," but I didn't care. He and I spent many happy hours with our sleds, making snowmen, and playing other innocent games.

Then there was the time when we broke the law, Ve and Rus and me, and thought, in our young minds, we were in grave danger of going to jail.

We had some friends who lived up the street from our rented house. The Testers were a nice young family, and we knew them before we came to Vegreville. Ve and I were disappointed that they had no girls, just two boys, but they were nice kids, and Rus was always happy to escape from two bossy sisters and enjoy some male playmates for a change.

On this particular evening, we had put on our overshoes, coats, toques, mittens, and scarves and walked the block or so to visit the Testers. We had a happy evening playing games in their warm and cozy home. Mama had told us to be home by nine o'clock, and we knew why. But the time raced along, and we were startled when Mrs. Tester told us to hurry and put on our things because there were just five minutes to nine.

Pure panic! We scrambled for our bulky winter gear, with our hostess helping. We practically knocked each other down in our haste to get home. Rus needed help in buckling his overshoes and, sensing his sisters' fright, began to cry. In our hurry we got garments on wrong and had to re-button and re-buckle.

We all got dressed in some fashion and shot out the back door, running for the lane as a shortcut. The alley was drifted high—no path and deep, deep snow. Through this icy moonlit landscape we stumbled, falling and floundering in our wild haste. Then we heard the town bell begin its nine o'clock reminder: Curfew! And we were not at home!

We were all bawling now. Rus was lagging behind, his short legs no match for the pristine drifts, and we all kept breaking through the snow-crust and becoming mired up to our waists.

The bell stopped. Snow-covered, absolutely exhausted, and frightened out of our wits that the town policeman would appear in the alley and grab us at any moment, we reached our back door and fell in, in a heap.

For the rest of our short stay in Vegreville, we avoided the kindly member of the R.C.M.P. who kept law and order in the town. If we saw him walking down the street, we lurked in doorways or hid behind fences. We knew we were fugitives from justice and could be picked up and charged at any time for breaking the curfew law.

That incident was very scary; getting lice was more painful than frightening. Mama couldn't help us in the drifted lane, but she knew what to do for head lice.

"Vera, go next door and ask Mrs. Smart if she has a fine-tooth comb. John, get the coal-oil can from the back porch. Russell, bring a big towel, and you, child, sit here in this chair."

I sat on the chair, scratching my head, swathed in a huge towel, while Mama hunted up a big handful of cotton batting. Ve had returned with Mrs. Smart, our motherly neighbour, in tow, as the delousing began.

Mama parted my hair in tiny wisps, combing out lice and shaking them onto a paper, which Mrs. Smart promptly fed into the firebox of our old cookstove. Then each tiny area of scalp was treated with a coal-oil-soaked ball of cottonwool. The air reeked of the pungent kerosene. I was howling, and Ve was busy telling Rus about lice and how I got them. Dear Mrs. Smart told me that it wasn't my fault at all, and Mama, during her vigorous treatment, also assured me that I couldn't help it.

The ordeal seemed to go on for a long time but was finally over. My head was wrapped in old rags and generously daubed with coal oil, and in this humiliating condition, I went to bed. Ve wouldn't sleep with me and moved to the front-room couch. I was lonely and forlorn, but finally fell asleep. In the middle of the night, I woke and threw up all over the bed, so poor Mama had another distasteful job.

About five A.M. she woke me up and ushered me back to the kitchen, where I got the shampoo of my life, with lots of yellow soap and hot water. Then I was seated in front of the open oven door to dry my hair before school. Mama said this whole painful procedure would have to be repeated in a few days, in order to get rid of any "nits" that might have hatched after my first treatment.

Still surrounded with a faint aura of "Essence of Coal Oil," I was aware of curious sniffs from the teacher and the other pupils in my class. My head no longer itched, but my scalp was sore for days.

Although other kids continued to pile their winter wear on top of mine in the cloakroom, I got no more lice. My toque and scarf seemed to retain a faint pungent smell. Most likely, the pesky vermin thought it was too life-threatening to meet up with my Mama and her delousing treatment!

22

Mama Makes Her Mark

We sat in the grass by the schoolyard's only flower bed, pulling leaves from the "old man" that struggled for existence there. The "old man" had survived during the summer vacation, when all our early flowers had thirsted for water and died. In spring Mrs. Bender had encouraged us to plant candytuft and nasturtiums and bachelor's-buttons. They had flourished until late June, when we had happily abandoned them with our traditional chant of "no more lessons, no more books, no more teacher's cross-eyed looks."

We were waiting for Mama and Papa to start for home now that they had voted. The school had seemed so still, so alien, as we stood at the back of the room and watched our parents perform this mysterious rite. It seemed so quick and simple, almost anticlimactic after all the election talk of the last few weeks.

The schoolroom still smelled of chalk and oiled floors and was cool after the August heat outside. The blackboards were clean, and all our handwriting specimens, maps, and artwork were gone from the walls. The framed portraits of King George and Queen Mary gazed steadily on us as they had done all the school year, but otherwise, the walls were clean and bare. Our desks remained in neat rows. No books or scribblers spilled from their open shelves.

Today Mr. Lawes sat at Mrs. Bender's desk with printed lists in front of him. George MacDonald had pulled up one of the larger pupils' desks and sat in it, putting a big tin box on its varnished top.

The cloakrooms were empty as we tiptoed in, our footsteps echoing hollowly off the wooden floors. Shy in the presence of the two unsmiling men, we remained silent as first Papa, then Mama, accepted the white slip of paper and disappeared behind the curtain in the chimney corner, then reappeared to slip the folded ballot into the waiting receptacle.

Now that our parents had voted, they were in no hurry to get back in the buggy for our return home. So we sat in the grass and scanned the road for other kids who might arrive with their parents. Mama and Papa were talking to Jim and Maggie Finnemore and Joe de Rosiers. For the first time in days, the conversation was not about the election but about crops and weather, the familiar components of our lives. It was as though—the ballot having finally been marked—things could now return to normal.

In the last few weeks, we had learned a lot of new words. Number one: "election"; Papa had patiently explained what it was and how it worked. That led to "candidate" and "vote," and the knowledge that certain men were "running." One candidate had actually visited the farm, but he didn't run up the dusty road as we had imagined he would. He came by in a shiny buggy pulled by two bay horses. Papa was summerfallowing in the south field when he came by, tied his horses to the barbed-wire fence, and painfully limped over the furrows, revealing himself to be quite lame and incapable of any sprinting at all. But Papa said he was "running" all right.

As "election day" neared, whenever a neighbour came over to bring the mail, borrow some machinery, or even passed by on the way to town, the talk turned to politics. Two farmers in lumber wagons, meeting on the rutted road, would rein in their teams and discuss taxes and election issues. If my sister and I and our little brother happened to be in the wagon, we soon became bored and climbed down to pick brown-eyed susans by the roadside or roll in the grass, until the men tired of the subject or suddenly remembered that the cows had to be milked before dark.

It was the same at home. When the old batches dropped by at suppertime and stayed for some of Mama's pounded steak and country gravy, it would start again. The men could talk of nothing else but the coming election.

Mama was quite uninterested in this talk. She would sit quietly, darning a sock or crocheting a doily, offering no opinions and looking extremely bored. On the infrequent occasions when neighbour women visited, the talk was of cooking and sewing, babies and gardens. Mama seemed to feel that politics was somehow unladylike. She fidgeted uncomfortably when the men's voices were raised in heated debate.

When Mrs. Wood sat in our front room and insisted on arguing with the men, Mama was quite disgusted. She was also unmoved when Papa kept reminding her that women now had the vote and that he expected her to go with him to the schoolhouse and make one more vote for "our man." She agreed to do that, but only to please him, not from any personal conviction.

But now that she had voted, she was lingering happily, visiting with neighbours, while we waited in the hot sun. A few more kids arrived with their parents. Ve strolled off with Karen Hoyem. I moved to follow, but they ordered me back. I was too young to share their secrets. I took Rus to the north side of the school, where we sat in the shade and sniffed at the ubiquitous weed that we called pineapple plant. If we pinched the tiny conical flowers, we were rewarded with a tangy pineapple perfume. Tiring of this, we joined several other young ones in a lazy game of I Spy. Then we played Duck on the Rock for a while, but the heat was too much for that, and we returned to the shade. Fed up with waiting, Rus ran to tug Papa's sleeve; he wanted to go home.

It seemed they were waiting until the votes were counted. Like Mama, a lot of women had come to vote for the first time, and this made the result particularly interesting. We were sure that Mama had voted right. Papa had questioned her again as we drove over in the buggy. He had coached her carefully, while we bumped along the narrow trail, thickly fringed with goldenrod and blue prairie asters.

"Remember, Myrtle, just put an X after the man's name. You know the one to vote for. Just one X, that's all."

"Prairie Women" 1989

"Yes, John. I know what to do. I hope Greta will remember to bring that apron pattern she promised me. There should be enough sandwiches for our lunch. I wonder if the Haeberles will bring the new baby." Mama rambled on with other topics.

When we finally drove home, we knew that our side had the most votes in that poll. Papa was very happy and even happier when Charlie Haeberle brought the news from town a few days later. "Our side" had won all over Alberta.

After election day, conversation went back to the topics of our workaday lives, but there was one comical incident on the Sunday that the Hansons came for dinner. At the table the talk turned again to the election. Papa said something about Mama's voting and joked that she had a lot to do with winning. Mama was all smiles.

"Easiest thing I ever did," she said, then added, "of course, the first X I made was for the wrong man. I was a little flustered, I suppose. But I stroked it out and finally got my X in the right place!"

Papa was lifting a bite of her delicious lemon pie to his mouth, and his fork seemed to stop in midair for a moment. Ole Hanson began to laugh but, noticing Papa's expression, thought better of it and busied himself with his cup and spoon.

Papa went on with his pie. Mama was puzzled.

"That was all right, wasn't it, John? I did vote for the right man, the one you told me to vote for."

"Never mind, Myrtle. I guess there's something I forgot to tell you." Papa began a conversation with Ole about the price of hogs.

Later that night, when the Hansons had gone home, we kids (and Mama) learned another new expression regarding elections: SPOILED BALLOT.

23

"Humouresque"

Joe de Rosiers put down his violin and started a very interesting conversation. Mama called Papa from the kitchen to hear it, and Ve and I left our paper dolls only half-dressed. There was no place for privacy in our little house, so we got to listen in on most adult talk. We were ordered outside sometimes, but that happened only in daylight and in summer. This was night and late October, so we heard the whole story. Rus was already in bed and asleep and would have to hear all this tomorrow.

Joe often brought his fiddle, and he and Mama would have a go at their music. Seems that practically the only tune Joe knew was "Humouresque," and he played it very badly. Mama wasn't the world's best accompanist either, and the result was pretty awful. That was the reason Papa had taken his *Free Press* into the kitchen. Over and over Joe sawed away, starting over whenever he hit a sour note. We were all thoroughly sick of "Humouresque," but Joe was not discouraged. Mama banged away, game as usual.

So we were glad when Joe put away the poor abused instrument and came up with his announcement. He blushed beet red as he began, and it was obvious that this was going to be pretty interesting. He was very embarrassed, looking down at his boots and mopping his brow with a big red hanky from time to time.

Joe had come to Alberta from Quebec. To us that was a faraway place, all the way across Canada on the big roll map at school. And, we had been told, everybody there spoke French. Joe did too, but we heard him speak a peculiar mixture of English and French. He tried hard. He was an earnest, serious young man who longed to master both the language and the violin.

Joe loved music. He had a favourite song too, and we kids were always amused when he broke into it. His choice, oddly, was "Mother Machree," and when he warbled, "There's a sput in me heart," we just dissolved into giggles. Joe didn't mind our laughter—he was fond of us, and we of him. He played games with us and taught us a little French, and we were proud of our limited vocabulary of familiar objects. He spent a lot of time at our place, away from his lonely shack on the prairie. He desperately wanted someone to share his life. Most of the marriageable girls around were snapped up into matrimony quickly, and so far, Joe had not been lucky.

So Joe's cousin René, down in Chicoutimi, recently married and joyful in domestic bliss, had found Joe a wife! A prospective wife, that is. Seems there was this girl, Marie, a neighbour of René and his wife. She was unmarried, of course, and didn't seem to have any suitors at the moment. René, ever aware of his cousin's single state, had been talking up Joe's charms and the adventure of moving out west to a new life.

René had written that Marie had seen a picture of Joe and had approved. Then, convinced by René's sales pitch, she had actually consented to get on the *train des voyageurs* and come out to Alberta and marry Joe!

René had also written that Marie was pretty (he sent a faded, dog-eared snap), very hard-working, good-natured, and adaptable—everything a man would want in a wife. The correspondence between the two cousins had been going on for a long time, but this decision had just recently been taken.

Joe's English got worse and he was talking almost entirely in French as he raved on and on about this wonderful girl whom he had never met, the joys of married life, and how he would never be *isolé* again. His blush deepened; he was actually perspiring. This wasn't an easy story for him to tell. The most startling announcement finally came out. Marie was coming in two weeks! Joe would meet the train in Bruce, they would be married right away, and we would soon be welcoming Mrs. Joe de Rosiers.

Ve and I were full of questions, but Mama shushed us and was quick with dozens of her own.

"How old is Marie?"

"Dix-neuf. How you say? Nineteen." Joe was thirty-two.

"Has Marie written to you, Joe?"

"Non. She cannot write so good. She hasn't been to school so much."

"Why?"

"She is an orphelin. She grow up in one of those places for poor leetle kids with no maman or papa. She have to work very hard since she just a leetle girl."

Now Mama got down to the practical stuff. "Joe," she said, "you haven't got much to offer this girl. Does she really know that you have only a poor farm, not much money, and a tiny two-room house?"

Mama was kind. Joe's "house" was really a shack, small, draughty, and incredibly dirty, as were most of the bachelors' places. We all knew this. We had seen Joe's place, and it was a mess.

Joe fielded all the questions with more optimism than practicality. Papa shrugged his shoulders and supposed it would all work out if the girl didn't expect too much. Mama suggested that the plan be changed. Why not bring Marie to our place for a little while before the marriage so the pair could get better acquainted? Joe became very sober at this—seems he had never doubted the wedding would come off! It was obvious to our parents that Joe wasn't much of a catch, but he was so happy and excited and elated by René's glowing description that his head was in the clouds. He was in love with Marie already or, maybe, in love with love. He finally agreed that the girl shouldn't be rushed. She would come and stay with us for a few days before the nuptials took place.

He went home whistling.

In the few days before Marie was due to arrive, we all embarked on a great flurry of activity. Joe's place had to be cleaned. Day after day, Mama bundled us kids into the buggy (luckily the snow had not come yet), and we drove over there with mops and brooms, old rags, and lots of soap. Joe had a big tub of hot water ready, and everyone scrubbed and polished and swept. Everything was dusted; windows were washed. Mama even brought some curtains, a refinement that had never appeared before in Joe's humble abode. We discovered that there were mice, and traps were set everywhere. Joe promised to get a cat right away!

Mama made a list of things that the prospective groom would have to buy. A frying pan and a coffee pot just weren't enough for a proper household.

When we got home at night, Mama would tell Papa that it was all so hopeless. Joe was going around with his head in the clouds, refusing to accept the reality of his new responsibilities and obligations. Papa just shook his head and kept telling Mama not to work so hard. Let Joe solve his own problems. Maybe the girl wouldn't expect too much and would just be happy to have a husband and some sort of home.

And so it went on, until the day that Marie was due to arrive in Bruce. On that morning Ford Merner, another bachelor, came by our place with his team and buggy on his way to town. He tied his team to the fence and came in to announce that Joe was sick with the flu, and he, Ford, was going to meet the train. After all this, poor Joe couldn't go to collect his Marie. Ford said Joe was pretty sick, and he didn't want to give his flu to his bride-to-be, so his friend would go for him. Since Marie was coming to our place anyway, the plan would hold, and in a few days, the couple could meet at last.

I guess the scene in Bruce when the train came in was pretty funny! Marie got off; Ford recognized her easily since there were only two other people who left the train, both men. Ford rushed to meet the girl, trying hard to explain in his almost non-existent French that he wasn't Joe. Marie didn't understand and threw her arms around the blushing bachelor, talking French like crazy. They finally got it sorted out with the help of Roland Dupré, the grain buyer, who was hanging around the station and who spoke a little French. Marie had two big trunks, which were loaded into the buggy, and the long drive began. They arrived at our place after dark.

We kids were still up—we had waited all day—and besides, Marie was to have our bed, and we would sleep on the floor again.

Marie at last. She was very weary and travel-worn, and she certainly wasn't pretty, as we had hoped she would be. She was a big girl, plain, raw-boned, with red, rough hands. No doubt that she worked very hard. We had an awkward time at first—she couldn't talk to us, and we couldn't talk to her—but Mama's kindness was evident without any conversation, and before long, we all found ways to communicate.

Marie and her trunks were installed in our tiny bedroom, Ford went home, and in the morning, we all awoke to a new day and a new situation: she turned out to be a real gem. She was a hard worker. Mama never had it so good as during her stay. She scrubbed and polished and made herself useful in dozens of ways. She could kill a chicken, pluck it, clean it, and cook it to perfection. She taught Mama to make tourtière. Her pea soup was wonderful; her pies and cakes were delicious. She even offered, in voluble French and with many gestures, to help Papa around the barn, an offer he declined. She played cat's cradle and hide-and-seek with Rus. She let Ve and me see the contents of her trunks, mostly sheets and towels and other nice linens. The poor girl had very few clothes, but she did have a hope chest of sorts.

We girls took it upon ourselves to help her with her English, and she seemed to improve every day.

Naturally, quite a few people had heard of our "French girl" and, even in very poor weather, came out of curiosity to see her. The old bachelors found many excuses to visit us, and Marie got plenty of attention. It was really comical to see them, much cleaner than usual, each trying his best to impress her.

Joe finally showed up, several days after the arrival of his prospective bride. He was pale and drawn; he really had been ill and hadn't "chickened out" as Papa had suspected. He was smitten at once and treated this sturdy girl like a very fragile china doll. They had long conversations in French. He played "Humouresque" for her. He took her to visit his place—they returned strangely silent. Did she not like what she saw? Neither one told us anything about their marriage plans.

With all the fellows around paying her compliments, which she had to understand by the way they were offered, Marie seemed to grow prettier every day, and we no longer looked on her as plain.

So we waited for the wedding. Ve and I asked Mama, asked Papa, asked Marie. "When is the wedding?" We could hardly wait. There would be a party for sure, and we loved parties. Papa asked Joe, and Joe seemed very uncomfortable and explained that Marie wanted more time. Marie had been with us two weeks. Papa was getting a little fed up with his crowded household and all the bachelors and Joe hanging around day after day.

Two weeks to Christmas. Everybody was pushing for a Christmas wedding.

Then suddenly, Marie went to work as a hired girl for Mrs. Clevely, an invalid who lived ten miles away. No explanation from her in French or English. No explanations from Joe.

Christmas came, and Joe had dinner with us as usual. Marie, he said, was still vacillating. She was kept busy at the Clevelys and sent a message that she would see us soon.

In January the weather was dreadful. Blizzards kept everyone away for weeks. School was over until March. We didn't even see Joe for all that month. February was no better. We really were marooned, and Papa nearly froze on his infrequent trips to town. We didn't have any news to speak of from any of the outlying farms. We kids kept busy making dozens of valentines and wondering who we could give them to.

Then, on a lovely, unseasonably warm day in March, a democrat, pulled by a glossy pair of bays, came in sight from the west. We knew the rig and the horses. On the front seat, flushed and happy, were a pair of newlyweds: Marie and Ford Merner!

We had the party after all. Lots of neighbours showed up. Even Joe, bearing a modest gift.

Joe took it very well. After an initial period of mourning, he went back to his "pre-Marie" existence. His shack degenerated into its former filthy state; he came over often and brought his fiddle. He played "Humouresque," and after a while, he was able to sing "Mother Machree" with his old enthusiasm.

24

You Can't Tell a Box by Its Cover

Mr. Hanson held the big box high and invited the men to start the bidding. It was a beautiful box, all pink-and-white ruffles and rosettes. Everybody in the room was sure it was Miss Murrow's. Joe de Rosiers started off the bids with a whopping five dollars!

Our little schoolhouse was packed for the box social. How different it looked at night. Even though two Aladdin's lamps had been pumped up and hung from the ceiling, there were still interesting shadows in the corners of the room. The blackboards had been cleaned off, and the big map rolled away. Miss Murrow had put up all our handwriting specimens and artwork for the parents to admire. The desks were all pushed to the walls and adults squeezed uncomfortably into the small seats that accommodated our skinny bottoms on school days. Two or three people had already got stains on their hands where inkwells had slopped.

The lamplight revealed our neighbours, dressed in their best clothes for the dance and auction. After a day spent in the fields, the men were well scrubbed but uncomfortable in unaccustomed starched collars and with fingernails that never seemed to come quite clean. Their wives, many of them wearing new dresses tediously homemade for this occasion, caught up on the local news between dances. Most of the women had marcelled hair, those precise waves achieved with a special iron, which was stuck in the glass globe of the coal-oil lamp until it was hot, then applied to the hair. All the kids were there, some of them already asleep in the cloakroom. Babysitters were unknown in our district, and all social gatherings included all the youngsters.

The dancing had stopped, and the musicians had put away their instruments until the auction and supper hour were over. It wasn't much of an orchestra: Ford Merner and his fiddle, Ole Hanson and his accordion, and various women alternating at chording on the organ.

While the grownups danced, we kids sneaked behind the makeshift curtains to stare at the boxes. Mrs. Lawes was guarding the table where the ladies had piled their offerings, and she was kept busy shoving away curious kids. The decorations on the boxes reflected the artistic ability of the creators. About the goodies inside, we could only guess. Papa had told Mama that he wanted to buy her box because he couldn't chance getting one put up by some bad cook.

Poor cooks were known all over the community. Their lack of skill at the stove was reported by all the bachelors, whose errands to neighbouring farms invariably coincided with mealtime. Mama was a good cook, and we always had lots of these "old batches" dropping by for her fried chicken and country gravy, sopped up with the airiest baking powder biscuits ever.

By the time the bidding started, we kids had been able to inspect the boxes pretty thoroughly. We had immediately classed the big pink-and-white one as Miss Murrow's. Who else could construct such a pretty effect with a hatbox and odds and ends of paper? Her box would be the prize catch.

Everybody adored the new teacher, who came after Mrs. Bender and her farmer husband moved away. She was young, pretty, and very popular with her pupils, their parents, and every single man for miles around. But she had no favourites. Mrs. Finney, who boarded the teacher, told people that Miss Murrow had a boyfriend in Edmonton. This bit of information was confirmed, just before the bidding started, by the arrival of a handsome young fellow who certainly seemed to be the teacher's beau. His clothes and general deportment marked him as a city man, and no one was surprised when Miss Murrow introduced him around as "my special friend,

Tom." This new rival spurred the local men to form a common front. They would have to prevent this city fellow from buying Miss Murrow's box!

So far the bidding had gone quite well. The shoe boxes covered with crepe paper and ribbon had been auctioned off one by one—the hobos' bindles, the grape baskets with multicoloured bows, the round boxes wrapped in hand-embroidered dishtowels, even a big bulky thing meant to look like a ship. Its masts had been broken on the way to the schoolhouse, and it looked more like a shipwreck.

Ve was very upset because the Strom twins, only fourteen, had brought boxes. They had been strutting around all night, wearing lipstick and tottering on high heels that they couldn't seem to control. Ve was fourteen too, and in the same grade as Ella and Eva Strom, yet Mama hadn't allowed her to bring a box, on the grounds that she was too young. Some of the fellows had asked her to dance, however, and she forgot her chagrin in the pleasure of these excursions out onto the powdered floor.

Nobody had asked me to dance, except Papa. He piloted my awkward eleven-year-old body around for one dance, and that was because I begged him to.

Every man in the room knew, to a cent, how much cash he had in his pockets, and if the bidding got beyond his budget, he was forced to drop out and try again on another offering. Most of the married men knew their wife's box and ended up with it. The single men were out to get the boxes of the single girls and maybe have a little fun with the married men by outbidding them on their wives' boxes. Even Lester, our young uncle, had got a box, a modest blue one with a red rose on the top. Lester felt lucky; he got the box for two dollars, and that was all the money he had.

The big pink-and-white box was the last one to be auctioned. Joe de Rosiers' five dollars was quickly topped by John Theaker at six. Miss Murrow's boyfriend bid seven. Joe came back with eight.

John Theaker had disgusted the women by coming to the dance in his overalls and dirty gumboots, but he had some money in those dirty pockets. He now bid nine. Tom, the boyfriend, bid nine-fifty. The bidding was getting tight, and some of the men were nervously counting their money. Ten dollars! That was a new bidder, Mac McLeod, the teacher from the neighbouring school district. But Mac didn't get it for his ten, and he had already bought one box, so that was his only bid. The bidders had narrowed to Joe, old John, and Tom. Joe bid eleven, Tom bid eleven-fifty, Joe bid twelve. John bid thirteen; Tom bid fourteen and gave up. Old John bid fifteen, and the bidding was over. Going once, going twice, going the third time at fifteen, chanted Mr. Hanson. Dirty John had got the teacher's box at fifteen dollars! Miss Murrow would have to eat supper with that filthy old bachelor who needed a bath and whose clothes reeked of the barnyard!

Time to open the boxes, examine the contents, and read the slip of paper with the lady's name. There were few surprises amongst the married couples, and Mr. and Mrs. generally shared her box.

But even in our unsophisticated little country community, fate could play some strange tricks. When the hidden names were revealed, it wasn't John Theaker who got Miss Murrow's box. He got Ella Strom's. That's right! One of the simpering Strom twins had somehow put together the beautiful creation with all the pink-and-white bows and flowers. She ate lunch with old John, making a poor attempt to hide her disgust. But she did have the glory of bringing in the evening's biggest bid. Joe de Rosiers didn't get a box; he had been so sure of getting the teacher's. Poor Tom bought one of Bud Lawes' boxes—he had two—and ate lunch with the other twin, Eva. A nice box it was, too, for the Stroms were dandy cooks.

Miss Murrow's box? Miss Murrow ate lunch with Lester, all pimples and embarrassment. Both were acutely aware that Lester had gotten into trouble at school that very day, and the teacher had been forced to keep him in.

Lester's two dollars had captured the prize box of the evening.

25

Holy Rollers

It was in Bruce that Ve and I "got religion." We didn't really, but we certainly became churchgoers for a time. Mama was pleased we were taking an interest in the church, but there was something Mama didn't know.

We spent three months in Bruce that winter—Mama, Ve, and I. As usual, we needed money, and when Papa went to town and learned that Russell Kennedy needed someone to help him, Mama was quick to apply for the job. Miss Olive, it seemed, was ill, and her brother was unable to cope with both the store and the post office. So Mama was hired to act as postmistress and to help in the general store until Miss Olive recovered.

We were installed in three rooms over an old vacant store, and Mama went out to work every day. Papa stayed on the farm to look after the livestock; Lester and Rus stayed with him. I guess Mama reasoned that the boys were better off with Papa and that Ve and I wouldn't supervise our little brother properly while she was toiling away at Kennedy's.

We had a great time in Bruce. Since the job was a temporary one, Mama didn't bother to put us in school. Our own school would reopen in March, and by that time, we would be back home. Every day we hurried through our assigned chores—hastily making the beds, doing the dishes, and dusting. Then we had nearly the whole day for fun.

We learned to skate. Every day we would lace on our second-hand boots, with blades as dull as hoes. We would wobble down the rickety stairs that led to the boardwalk, worn and uneven, with plenty of cracks, on the street. Getting to the pond was quite an achievement, and sometimes when we got there, our small and bumpy "skating rink" was covered with fresh snow, which we had to sweep off. With ankles turning in and out and many a fall, we floundered around until we got some mastery of the awkward blades.

The pond was close to the railroad station; the local, the flyer, the freight trains, and even an occasional silk train were welcome diversions. Of course, we counted the freight cars and were delighted when the caboose rattled by and some of the crew waved back.

During the day we would drop in to Kennedy's, proud to see Mama efficiently handing out the mail and selling stamps, money orders, and postal notes. This was a side of our mother we had never seen before. We also soon learned that if we dropped in to say hello to sweet old Hop Sing in his little store, he was bound to give us a chocolate drop or some other candy.

The old couple across the street had a new thing they called a radio, and they invited us in to hear this newfangled invention. It was a bulky, black box with knobs and wires and big batteries. We put on the earphones and listened to a lot of squawks and squeals and, sometimes, some tinny music. The old fellow kept twiddling the dials to get what he called "better reception." We soon lost interest in the radio, but continued to visit for the doughnuts and milk that the dear old lady provided.

There was a dance at the school every Saturday night, and we always attended. A very genial fellow named Mr. Barker led the band and organized singsongs. Mama enjoyed the dancing, and we girls, being too young to dance, looked forward to the singing.

Papa and the boys came to Bruce once in a while, but found the trip very difficult—there were lots of snowstorms and bad weather that winter.

We found lots to do during the day, but we were really waiting for the Fredericks' kids to get out of school. Almost as soon as we had settled into our temporary home, we had struck up a friendship with the Fredericks. There were four of them, roughly our ages; two girls and two boys. Their mother was warm and friendly, and we were always welcome in their home. We spent many happy hours around that big, round kitchen table, playing cards and other games and stuffing ourselves with popcorn and peanuts.

It was the Fredericks kids who led us to the church and our religious experience. At home we never went to church because there wasn't one. Mama and Papa would love to have attended, and did on the very rare occasion when some preacher came out to Rutherglen.

Mama readily gave her permission when we asked to go to Sunday evening services, but decided not to go herself as it wasn't her church. Mr. and Mrs. Fredericks didn't go either, only the children.

"What kind of church is it?"

"Oh, they're Holy Rollers."

We had never heard of such a church.

"It's great fun. We're waiting to see them roll."

"Do they really do that?"

"They sure do, but we haven't seen them yet. We're going every Sunday and waiting 'til they do it."

So every Sunday, seven o'clock, we buckled on our overshoes, put on our mittens, toques, and scarves and waded through the drifts to the tiny church on the edge of town. Of course, the church wasn't called "Holy Roller"; it was just a small flock of Free Methodists.

We lined ourselves up in the very back pew, ready to wait it out until the rolling started. Six giggling, elbow-nudging, noisy kids. Six pairs of watchful eyes, ever scanning the congregation for any sign of the performance we had come to see. We shouted out the hymns at the top of our lungs, provoking frowns and disapproving looks from the adults around us. The small assembly was quiet and reverent.

Once in a while some mother would slip to the back of the room to nurse her baby, and we found this natural and beautiful action hilarious for some reason. One after another, we would turn and stare at her. More giggles.

We then became "rollers," though not necessarily holy. Somehow we discovered that a marble, if launched from a back pew, would roll very satisfactorily to the front of the church, to rest, we hoped at the altar. The poor young preacher would pause in the middle of his earnest sermon, suddenly aware that most of his congregation was watching a big coloured alley slowly rolling down the aisle. Flustered, he would push on, even though the giggles at the back were audible.

We kept this up for several weeks. I will never know why that nice man of God didn't throw us out! The good folk of the church never "rolled" or acted any differently from any other churchgoers.

Someone finally went into the post office and told Mama what we kids were up to on Sunday nights and why we had become such regular churchgoers. Mama went to see Mrs. Fredericks, and from then on, we spent our Sunday evenings at home or playing games at the Fredericks' house.

Miss Olive got better. We went back to the farm. And the only "Holy Rollers" proved to be us.

26

Ride ’em, Cowgirl

Before the advent of the Haeberles, we were content to be farm children. We accepted the yearly cycles of tilling, sowing, and reaping; the chores of milking and feeding chickens and hogs were normal and even interesting.

When the property to the north was settled, though, we realized at last that life had its options. The Haeberles weren’t farmers at all—they were cowboys. They came from “down south,” wherever that was, and they had no intention of growing crops. They intended to raise cattle.

In the business of “running a herd,” some equestrian skills are necessary, so Charlie Haeberle brought along a couple of cowboys to help with the roping, branding, and herding. Young Bill was already pretty handy with a lariat, and the Haeberles’ back lot was a busy place as the horsemen roped and tied and “broke in” rebellious broncos.

Charlie was a real cowboy, with bowed legs and a face that was as brown and shiny as his favourite saddle. He wore chaps and a big brown western hat. He entered nearly every competition at the Bruce Stampede and won lots of prizes. He wasn’t handsome, but he was glamourous. We three kids sat on the top rail of the Haeberle corral and watched the activity inside with much interest. This was the life! We would be cowboys too.

We were quite young then and weren’t allowed to ride Papa’s saddle horse, so we had built up a stable of stick horses, which we rode everywhere around the farm. These humble steeds had names and were stabled and groomed continually. We must have been a comical sight astride these sticks as we galloped madly from bluff to bluff and raced our mounts on the dusty roads. We also rode the calves in the calf pen for a while, but Mama discouraged that after Ve fell off one of the frisky young steers and got her face stepped on. They were silly things anyway, stampeding whenever Rover barked at them.

After the Haeberles came, we discarded our poor sticks as ridiculous and began to pester Papa for real horses. Papa had only two ponies, besides the work horses. Nellie was his saddle horse and considered too high-strung for us, although Ve was sometimes allowed to ride her. I had to settle for old Buck, whose proper function was to pull the buggy. However, in my ambition to become a cowgirl, fate played into my hands. That year Ve wasn't attending school, and Rus hadn't started yet, so I had to go alone and ride old Buck. This was perfect. Alone on the prairie, I could perfect my techniques and emerge as a skilled rider.

Every morning I saddled my old blue roan and set off for school, a dumpy twelve-year-old on a reluctant horse that moved at a sedate walk or, at best, a slow trot.

Every morning Papa warned me not to try to gallop old Buck.

"Remember, you keep him at a trot. He stumbles if he tries to go any faster."

"Yes, Papa, I'll remember."

Out of sight of the farmhouse, a metamorphosis took place. No longer was I a lumpish schoolgirl on a tired old nag, but a dashing cowgirl on a fiery bucking horse. In my imagination my chaps were the gayest imaginable, my white hat shaded my eyes, and those bare heels that dug into my horse's flanks were really encased in hand-tooled boots with high heels and twinkling silver spurs. Old Buck wasn't slow or unwilling, but "rarin' to go"—a snorting, unmanageable piece of horseflesh that only I could control.

But the reality was most discouraging to an aspiring rodeo star. Buck did stumble, regularly. His short bursts of speed always ended the same way, with me sitting on the prairie and him standing by, patiently waiting for me to mount him again. This I would do in complete frustration, muttering my disappointment that Papa wouldn't give me a better pony to ride. If I could have Nellie, I would soon be a dandy rider and the envy of all my friends. I could even go horseback riding with Billy Haeberle. The thought of handsome young Bill led me to the realization that maybe he was the real reason for my ambition. Billy would surely notice a girl who was handy with a horse and a rope.

So I would climb back on my sluggish steed and continue on to school, only to try again tomorrow. Surely Buck could learn to gallop without both of us ending up in this embarrassing sprawl every time.

School was out for another day. Old Buck and I went through our daily routine of saddling up. Every time I tried to cinch the girth, he expanded his belly to an enormous size while I pulled and tugged at the strap to make it tight. Then, the cinching over, my horse would return to his normal size, and when I put my foot in the stirrup, the saddle would turn around and hang below him. This happened every day. My wise old horse knew he was dealing with an innocent. But finally, after much struggle and a knee in his side, he gave up, and I was able to start home.

A lovely afternoon. Maybe a little gallop?

All went well until we came to the dry slough bottom. It was rough and hard, and of course, my horse stumbled. Instead of me landing clear with him standing by, he landed on top of me this time.

Old Buck floundered and gained his feet. As usual he waited for me to get back in the saddle. But this time I couldn't rise. My leg! It was surely broken. I tried to stand, but the pain brought me back to the stony ground. I groaned in agony. My horse made no attempt to leave me and started to crop the grass around him.

Along with the pain of my broken leg—I was sure it was broken—was the realization that I would soon be expected home from school. Mama would worry, while Papa would be sure to guess what had happened. Now that I had really gotten into trouble, I lay on the unyielding clay and vowed that from now on I would keep to a slow trot.

The sound of approaching horses. Two riders appeared over the rise and shouted with surprise as they saw my predicament. Raising my head to ask for help, my physical pain was joined with acute embarrassment, for one of the approaching pair was Billy Haeberle. His companion was a beautiful young girl who handled her mount with all the skill I lacked.

They bundled me on my horse and led us home. On the way I learned that the girl was Billy's cousin, Patsy, up from southern Alberta on a visit. Before we reached our gate, I was aware that she had probably learned to ride about the same time she learned to walk. They were very kind and sympathetic, as professionals to a clumsy amateur, and somehow their concern added to my misery.

Mama had to leave supper on the stove and drive me to town. Old Doc Storey gave the leg a thorough examination and announced that luckily it was not broken, only badly bruised.

While I was out of school, limping around on my black-and-blue leg, I often saw Billy and Patsy racing by on their ponies. Sometimes they stopped by to ask about me.

When the worst was over, Buck and I continued to go to school, at a sedate trot or a fast walk. Both of us knew our limitations.

In the fall, we left the farm. Old Buck and I had to part. He was probably glad. He wasn't cut out to be a rodeo horse.

27

In the Swim of Things

It happened just before we moved to town. Since our trips to Viking were generally hurried affairs, we knew no other kids, just some of the storekeepers and a few adults whom our parents dealt with.

Now that we were going to live there, though, we were learning more about the town all the time, and before long, we became aware that there was a lake. Right away we wanted to go to this lake, learn to swim, and maybe meet some of the town kids. We pestered Mama and Papa to please take us to the lake, and they finally promised that one day this summer we would all go.

It needed some preparation. Number one: we would have to get some bathing suits. On our berry-picking trips to Birch Lake, we children had tested the water in the narrow channel at the south end of the island. Ve and I had ventured into these shallow waters in our panties, Rus in his underdrawers. That wouldn't do if we were at Lake Thomas with the town crowd, so we all got bathing costumes from Eaton's. Ours were navy blue cotton jersey with red trim. Thinking back, they were awful, but we didn't know that then. Even Mama and Papa got proper attire, and as I remember, theirs were wool. Mama's was a blue heather mixture; Papa's was brown. They were all one-piecers, extremely modest.

The expenditure was justified on the grounds that now we would be living in the town, we would go to the lake a lot, learn to swim, and be right in style with those lucky town-dwellers.

The day finally came. A lovely, sunny Sunday. Joe de Rosiers promised to milk the cows and feed the horses so we could have a nice long day, and we set out early with our picnic lunch.

There were a lot of people out to enjoy the water. Lake Thomas was known to have a high salt content, so the water was very buoyant. On a nice warm day like this one, many people were taking advantage of its delights. Families were spread all over the grass; there were many waders at the water's edge and quite a few swimmers.

Ve and I quickly spotted the darling little bathhouses, where we could get into our new suits. Ours had a nice little bench attached to the walls and hooks to hang things on. There was no floor, just the ground, but we were charmed to find we wouldn't have to change in the car.

Oh, we had a marvellous time. I quickly discovered that learning to swim was easy; so did Ve. Rus was a little nervous and spent his time mostly wading near the shore. Papa struck way out—he had learned to swim long ago. Mama didn't do much except sit on shore (it really couldn't be called a beach), nervously watching her offspring because someone had told her of dangerous drops in the lake bottom not far from the water line.

We shyly exchanged a few words with other girls. This was great! New friends, a new accomplishment, and soon, we would live in town and go to the lake all the time! No longer farm kids, we would be in with the crowd, sophisticated swimmers, spending our spare time at Lake Thomas. I thrashed about, practising my swimming. What fun! I didn't notice the black clouds gathering. The wind was rising too, but I didn't care. Some people were leaving the water. Mama called loudly from the shore, telling us to get out, and hurry. Ve, always obedient, left and ran up the grass to the bathhouse. Mama called again, and I begged for just a few more minutes.

"Come at once. There is going to be a storm!" Now I could see waves rising everywhere. The clouds really were menacing.

Reluctantly, I left the water and took off for the little shack. Papa had joined Mama in urging me to hurry, hurry. Now I

"Reunion"

ran, got into the bathhouse, and as the storm struck and the wind rose, stripped off my soggy suit. As I reached for my towel and clothes, the gale rocked the tiny structure. Suddenly, a strong gust lifted the whole bathhouse, leaving me standing naked on the prairie. To my horror, at the same time I saw a granary in a nearby field go sailing through the air.

So there I stood, absolutely bare, my clothes and towel gone, as people ran every which way around me. I took to my heels and ran for a nearby clump of willow. Here I cowered, frantically trying to pull the trees around me as the wind whipped my leafy retreat.

The rest of the family, safe in the car, had witnessed my humiliating predicament. Papa came with a blanket and, my modesty restored, escorted me through the gale to a safe and less conspicuous place.

The storm was over almost as quickly as it had hit. Having sat it out in the Chevy, we were unhurt, although I had a lot of scratches from the willows. Only my dignity was seriously injured.

The bathhouse was shattered and ended up a quarter-mile away. My soggy clothing, including my new bathing suit, was scattered far and wide. We never did find my dress. We moved to town a few weeks later and were much too busy to go to the lake.

It was a family joke that I was a very poor runner, coming in last in practically every footrace I ever ran. But that day at Lake Thomas, I was fast—really fast!

28

Goodbye to the Farm

Life in town would be very exciting, we told each other. We would have a big house, our own bedrooms, an upstairs, a gas stove, and a radiant-gas fireplace in the parlour. There would be gas lamps and a real sink in the kitchen. We would be going to the big school, where they had five teachers. Imagine! We would just have to walk out the back door, past the creamery, cut across a vacant lot, and we would be at the school. There would be new friends, new activities, a whole new way of life.

Mama and Papa had given up on the farm. A series of natural disasters, coupled with the general unproductiveness of the soil and other discouraging factors, had forced a decision.

For three years we had been hailed out. Early frost took whatever the hail missed. Ve and I were both ready to start high school; Rus hadn't started grade one yet. Our parents spent the evenings discussing the hopeless situation and finally made their plans. Papa was a pretty good carpenter; Mama would take in boarders. The creamery manager had a good farm close to town, and if the carpentry work failed to appear, Papa would work it for wages, with no risk involved.

So it was goodbye to the farm. Goodbye to the log house where I was born. Goodbye to Tidy's Hill, where the first crocuses peeked out in spring. Goodbye to Rosie's, Jake's place, and all the other bluffs we named when we stabled our stick horses there.

Goodbye to the north pasture, where the mushrooms sprang up after a summer shower. Goodbye to bare feet in the soft summer grass.

Goodbye to the windmill and its platform, where I crawled when I was only two years old and gave Mama fits. Goodbye to the barn with its mangers full of sweet-smelling hay and the soft sounds of the horses at night. Goodbye to the chicken house, where Mama had optimistically raised white leghorns, until they all died with some mysterious chicken disease.

Would the pleasures of the town make up for the wild roses and the big strawberries that grew on the prairie? Rover and Buff would be going with us, but how about the horses, the cows, and the soft-eyed young calves?

One by one and piece by piece, the animals and farm machinery were sold. Finally there was only old Buck left; no one wanted the poor old blue roan. Papa practically had to give him away to the Otto family, where he was to start a new career hauling their kids to school.

I put my arms around my horse's neck and remembered all the times he had stumbled and fallen on the way to school, leaving me sitting on the grass. But he never left me, always waiting for me to get back up on his back. Many times I had brushed the mosquitoes from his sturdy neck, oblivious to the fact that I too was being bitten by the nasty little pests. When Mr. Otto's eldest boy came to lead Buck away to his new home, I wept as though my heart would break.

But we didn't waste much time crying for our life on the farm. Although there was nothing left except our dog and our cat and our furniture, we left with high hopes for a new life.

With our modest belongings packed for moving, the little house was revealed as it really was—a poor, draughty, inconvenient little abode—no longer a home. It was not the surroundings that made it a happy, cosy, secure haven. It was the loving parents who struggled so mightily against the capricious forces of nature, finally abandoning the fight for the sake of their three children.